BITCOIN DEVELOPMENT PHILOSOPHY

Kalle & Linnéa Rosenbaum

KONSENSUS NETWORK

chaincode

Edited by Marta Turchetta

Cover design and typesetting by Konsensus Network

ISBN 978-9916-723-58-6 Hardcover

   978-9916-723-59-3 Paperback

   978-9916-723-60-9 E-book

KONSENSUS NETWORK ★ https://konsensus.network

To the relentless innovators and pioneers of Bitcoin development, whose passion and commitment to building decentralized and trustless systems have paved the way for a new era of financial sovereignty and freedom. This work is a tribute to their endeavors and a contribution to the continuous development and understanding of Bitcoin.

CONTENTS

FOREWORD

The realm of Bitcoin is vast, housing within its domains various concepts, processes, and systems that are both revolutionary and intricate. It demands not just technical acuity but a holistic understanding of its fundamental principles and inherent trade-offs. Bitcoin Development Philosophy seeks to journey through this realm, unraveling the different aspects of Bitcoin, and serving as a guide for those who wish to delve into the complex world of Bitcoin protocol development. It is a guide, a companion, and a lens through which the significance of Bitcoin can be appreciated in its full spectrum.

PREFACE

Bitcoin Development Philosophy is a contemplative exploration into the very essence of Bitcoin. It aims to equip developers with a good understanding of the philosophical underpinnings and design paradigms of Bitcoin, enabling them to navigate its complex realms with informed discretion and curiosity. This book is the culmination of lessons learned over a decade of Bitcoin development and public debate, designed to provide context and clarity to both seasoned and novice developers.

Acknowledgements

Our profound gratitude to *Chaincode Labs* for commissioning and funding this insightful piece of work and to every individual who contributed their insights and expertise in the making of this guide. We extend our heartfelt thanks to Kalle Rosenbaum, the main author, and Linnéa Rosenbaum, the co-author, whose invaluable insights and efforts have shaped this book. The pursuit of knowledge is a collective endeavor, and this work is imbued with the wisdom and experiences of many brilliant minds from the Bitcoin development community.

1

DECENTRALIZATION

This chapter analyzes what decentralization is and why it's essential for Bitcoin to function. We distinguish between the decentralization of miners and that of full nodes, and discuss what they bring to the table for censorship resistance, one of Bitcoin's most central properties. The discussion then shifts to understanding neutrality - or permissionlessness towards users, miners, and developers - which is a necessary property of any decentralized system. Lastly, we touch upon how hard it can be to grasp a decentralized system like Bitcoin, and present some mental models that might help you grok it.

A system without any central point of control is referred to as being *decentralized*. Bitcoin is designed to avoid having a central point of control, or more precisely a *central point of censorship*. Decentralization is a means to achieve *censorship resistance*.

There are two major aspects of decentralization in Bitcoin: miner decentralization and full node decentralization. Miner decentralization refers to the fact that transaction processing isn't performed nor coordinated by any central entity. Full node decentralization refers to the fact that validation of the blocks, i.e. the data that miners output, gets done at the edge of the network, ultimately by its users, and not by a few trusted authorities.

Miner decentralization

There had been attempts at creating digital currencies before Bitcoin, but most of them failed due to a lack of governance decentralization and censorship resistance.

Miner decentralization in Bitcoin means that the *ordering of transactions* isn't carried out by any single entity or fixed set of entities. It's carried out collectively by all the actors who want to participate in it; this miners' collective is a dynamic set of users. Anyone can join or leave as they wish. This property makes Bitcoin censorship-resistant.

If Bitcoin were centralized, it would be vulnerable to those who wished to censor it, such as governments. It would meet the same fate as earlier attempts to create digital money. In the introduction of a paper titled "Enabling Blockchain Innovations with Pegged Sidechains", the authors explain how early versions of digital money weren't equipped for an adversarial environment (see also Adversarial thinking):

David Chaum introduced digital cash as a research topic in 1983, in a setting with a central server that is trusted to prevent double-spending[Cha83]. To mitigate the privacy risk to individuals from this central trusted party, and to enforce fungibility, Chaum introduced the blind signature, which he used to provide a cryptographic means to prevent linking of the central server's signatures (which represent coins), while still allowing the central server to perform double-spend prevention. The requirement for a central server became the Achilles' heel of digital cash[Gri99]. While it is possible to distribute this single point of failure by replacing the central server's signature with a threshold signature of several signers, it is important for auditability that the signers be distinct and identifiable. This still leaves the system vulnerable to failure, since each signer can fail, or be made to fail, one by one.

— Enabling Blockchain Innovations with Pegged Sidechains (2014)

It became clear that using a central server to order transactions was not a viable option due to the high risk of censorship. Even if one replaced the central server with a federation of a fixed set of n servers, of which at least m must approve of an ordering, there would still be difficulties. The problem would indeed shift to one where users must agree on this set of n servers as well as on how to replace malicious servers with good ones without relying on a central authority.

Let's contemplate what could happen if Bitcoin were censorable. The censor could pressure users to identify themselves, to declare where their money is coming from or what they're buying with it before allowing their transactions to enter the blockchain.

Also, the lack of censorship resistance would allow the censor to coerce users into adopting new system rules. For example, they could impose a change that allowed them to inflate the money supply, thereby enriching themselves. In such an event, a user verifying blocks would have three options to handle the new rules:

- Adopt: Accept the changes and adopt them into their full node.

- Reject: Refuse to adopt the changes; this leaves the user with a system that doesn't process transactions anymore, as the censor's blocks are now deemed invalid by the user's full node.

- Move: Appoint a new central point of control; all of the users must figure out how to coordinate and then agree on the new central control point. If they succeed, the same issues will most likely resurface at some point in the future, considering that the system remained just as censorable as it was before.

None of these options are beneficial to the user.

Censorship resistance through decentralization is what separates Bitcoin from other money systems, but it is not an easy thing to accomplish due to the *double-spending problem*. This is the problem of making sure no one can spend the same coin twice, an issue that many people thought was impossible to solve in a decentralized fashion. Satoshi Nakamoto write in his Bitcoin whitepaper about how to solve the double-spending problem:

> *In this paper, we propose a solution to the double-spending problem using a peer-to-peer distributed timestamp server to generate computational proof of the chronological order of transactions.*
> — *Satoshi Nakamoto – Bitcoin: A Peer-to-Peer Electronic Cash System (2008)*

Here he uses the peculiar-sounding phrase "peer-to-peer distributed timestamp server". The keyword here is *distributed*, which in this context means that there is no central point of control. Nakamoto then goes on to explain how proof-of-work is the solution. Still, no one explains it better than Gregory Maxwell on Reddit, where he responds to someone who proposes to limit miners' hash power to avoid potential 51% attacks:

> *A decentralized system like Bitcoin uses a public election. But you can't just have a vote of 'people' in a decentralized system because that would require a centralized party to authorize people to vote. Instead, Bitcoin uses a vote of computing power because it's possible to verify computing power without the help of any centralized third party.*
>
> — *Gregory Maxwell – r/Bitcoin subreddit (2019)*

The post explains how the decentralized Bitcoin network can come to an agreement on transaction ordering through the use of proof-of-work. He then concludes by saying that the 51% attack is not particularly worrisome, compared to people not caring about or not understanding Bitcoin's decentralization properties.

> *A far bigger risk to Bitcoin is that the public using it won't understand, won't care, and won't protect the decentralization properties that make it valuable over centralized alternatives in the first place.*
>
> — *Gregory Maxwell – r/Bitcoin subreddit (2019)*

The conclusion is an important one. If people don't protect Bitcoin's decentralization, which is a proxy for its censorship resistance, Bitcoin might fall victim to centralizing powers, until it's so centralized that censorship becomes a thing. Then most, if not all, of its value proposition is gone. This brings us to the next section on full node decentralization.

Full node decentralization

In the paragraphs above, we've mostly talked about miner decentralization and how centralizating miners can allow for censorship. But there's also another aspect of decentralization, namely *full node decentralization*.

The importance of full node decentralization is related to trustlessness (see Trustlessness). Suppose a user stops running their own full node due to, for example, a prohibitive increase in the cost of operation. In that case, they have to interact with the Bitcoin network in some other way, possibly by using web wallets or lightweight wallets, which requires a certain level of trust in the providers of these services. The user goes from directly enforcing the network consensus rules to trusting that someone else will. Now suppose that most users delegate consensus enforcement to a trusted entity. In that case, the network can quickly spiral into centralization, and the network rules can be changed by conspiring malicious actors.

In a Bitcoin Magazine article, Aaron van Wirdum interviews Bitcoin developers about their views on decentralization and the risks involved in increasing Bitcoin's maximum block size. This discussion was a hot topic during the 2014-2017 era, when many people argued over increasing the block size limit to allow for more transaction throughput.

A powerful argument against increasing the block size is that it increases the cost of verification (see the Scaling chapter). If verification cost rises, it will push some users to stop running their full nodes. This, in turn, will lead to more people not being able to use the system in a trustless way. Pieter Wuille is quoted in the article, where he explains the risks of full node centralization.

If lots companies run a full node, it means they all need to be convinced to implement a different rule set. In other words: the decentralization of block validation is what gives consensus rules their weight. But if full node count would drop very low, for instance because everyone uses the same web-wallets, exchanges and SPV or mobile wallets, regulation could become a reality. And if authorities can regulate the consensus rules, it means they can change anything that makes Bitcoin Bitcoin. Even the 21 million bitcoin limit.

— Pieter Wuille – The Decentralist Perspective or Why Bitcoin Might Need Small Blocks (2015)

There you go. Bitcoin users should run their own full nodes to deter regulators and big corporations from trying to change the consensus rules.

Neutrality

Bitcoin is neutral, or permissionless, as people like to call it. This means that Bitcoin doesn't care who you are or what you use it for.

bitcoin is neutral, which is a good thing, and the only way it can work. if it was controlled by an organisation it'd just be another virtual object type and I would have zero interest in it

— wumpus on freenode IRC (punctuation added) #bitcoin-core-dev 2012-04-04T17:34:04 UTC

As long as you play by the rules, you're free to use it as you please, without asking anyone for permission. This includes *mining, transacting* in, and *building protocols and services* on top of Bitcoin.

- If **mining** were a permissioned process, we would need a central authority to select who's allowed to mine. This would most likely lead to miners having to sign legal contracts in which they would agree to censor transactions according to the whims of the central authority, which defeats the purpose of mining in the first place.

- If people **transacting** in Bitcoin had to provide personal information, declare what their transactions were for, or otherwise prove that they were worthy of transacting, we would also need a central point of authority to approve users or transactions. Again, this would lead to censorship and exclusion.

- If developers had to ask for permission to **build protocols** on top of Bitcoin, only the protocols allowed by the central developer granting committee would get developed. This would, due to government intervention, inevitably exclude all privacy-preserving protocols and all attempts at improving decentralization.

At all levels, trying to impose restrictions on who gets to use Bitcoin for what will hurt Bitcoin to the point where it's no longer living up to its value proposition.

Pieter   Wuille   answers a question on Stack Exchange   about   how the blockchain relates to normal databases. He explains how permissionlessness is achievable through the use of proof-of-work in combination with economic incentives. He concludes:

> *Using trustless consensus algorithms like PoW does add something no other construction gives you (permissionless participation, meaning there is no set group of participants that can censor your changes), but comes at a high cost, and its economic assumptions make it pretty much only useful for systems that define their*

own cryptocurrency. There is probably only place in the world for one or a few actually used ones of these.

— *Pieter Wuille – Stack Exchange (2019)*

He explains that, in order to achieve permissionlessness, the system most likely needs its own currency, thereby "limiting the use cases to effectively just cryptocurrencies". This is because permissionless participation, or mining, requires economic incentives built into the system itself.

Grokking decentralization

A compelling aspect of Bitcoin is how hard it is to grasp that no one controls it. There are no committees or executives in Bitcoin. Gregory Maxwell, again on the Bitcoin subreddit, compares this to the English language in an intriguing way:

> *Many people have a hard time understanding autonomous systems, there are many in their lives things like the english language-- but people just take them for granted and don't even think of them as systems. They're stuck in a centralized way of thinking where everything they think of as a 'thing' has an authority that controls it.*
>
> *Bitcoin doesn't focus on anything. Various people who have adopted Bitcoin chose of their own free will to promote it, and how they choose to do so is their own business. Authority fixated people may see these activities and believe they're some operation by the bitcoin authority, but no such authority exists.*
>
> — *Gregory Maxwell – r/Bitcoin subreddit (2022)*

The way Bitcoin works through decentralization resembles the extraordinary collective intelligence found among many species in nature. Com-

Figure 1.1: Fish schools have no leaders.

puter scientist Radhika Nagpal speaks in a Ted talk about the collective behavior of fish schools and how scientists are trying to mimic it using robots.

> *Secondly, and the thing that I still find most remarkable, is that we know that there are no leaders supervising this fish school. Instead, this incredible collective mind behavior is emerging purely from the interactions of one fish and another. Somehow, there are these interactions or rules of engagement between neighboring fish that make it all work out.*
>
> *— Radhika Nagpal – What intelligent machines can learn from a school of fish (2017)*

She points out that many systems, either natural or artificial, can and do work without leaders, and they are powerful and resilient. Each individual only interacts with their immediate surroundings, but together they form something tremendous.

No matter what you think about Bitcoin, its decentralized nature makes it difficult to control. Bitcoin exists, and there's nothing you can do about it. It's something to be studied, not debated.

Conclusion

We distinguish between full node decentralization and mining decentralization. Mining decentralization is a means to achieve censonship resistance, while full node decentralization is what keeps the consensus rules of the network hard to change without broad support among users.

The decentralized nature of Bitcoin allows for neutrality towards developers, users, and miners. Anyone is free to participate without asking for permission.

Decentralized systems can be hard to wrap your head around, but there are some mental models that may help, for example the English language, or fish schools.

2

TRUSTLESSNESS

This chapter dissects the concept of trustlessness, what it means from a computer science perspective, and why Bitcoin has to be trustless to retain its value proposition. We then talk about what it means to use Bitcoin in a trustless way, and what kind of guarantees a full node can and cannot give you. In the last section, we look at the real-world interaction between Bitcoin and actual softwares or users, and the need to make trade-offs between convenience and trustlessness to get anything done at all.

People often say things like "Bitcoin is great because it's trustless". What do they mean by trustless? Pieter Wuille explains this widely used term on Stack Exchange:

> *The trust we're talking about in "trustless" is an abstract technical term. A distributed system is called trustless when it does not require any trusted parties to function correctly.*
>
> — *Pieter Wuille – Bitcoin Stack Exchange (2016)*

In short, the word *trustless* refers to a property of the Bitcoin protocol whereby it can logically function without "any trusted parties". This is different from the trust you inevitably have to put into the software or hardware you run. More on this latter aspect of trust will be discussed further in this chapter.

In centralized systems, we rely on a central actor's reputation in order to make sure that they will take care of security or roll back in case of issues, as well as on the legal system to sanction any violations. These trust requirements are problematic in pseudonymous decentralized systems - there is no possibility of recourse so there really can't be any trust. In the introduction to the Bitcoin whitepaper, Satoshi Nakamoto describes this problem:

Commerce on the Internet has come to rely almost exclusively on financial institutions serving as trusted third parties to process electronic payments. While the system works well enough for most transactions, it still suffers from the inherent weaknesses of the trust based model. Completely non-reversible transactions are not really possible, since financial institutions cannot avoid mediating disputes. The cost of mediation increases transaction costs, limiting the minimum practical transaction size and cutting off the possibility for small casual transactions, and there is a broader cost in the loss of ability to make non-reversible payments for nonreversible services. With the possibility of reversal, the need for trust spreads. Merchants must be wary of their customers, hassling them for more information than they would otherwise need. A certain percentage of fraud is accepted as unavoidable. These costs and payment uncertainties can be avoided in person by using physical currency, but no mechanism exists to make payments over a communications channel without a trusted party

— Satoshi Nakamoto – Bitcoin: A Peer-to-Peer Electronic Cash System (2008)

It seems that we can't have a decentralized system based on trust, and that's why trustlessness is important in Bitcoin.

To use Bitcoin in a trustless manner, you have to run a fully-validating Bitcoin node. Only then will you be able to verify that the blocks you receive from others are following the consensus rules; for example, that the coin issuance schedule is kept and that no double-spends occur on the blockchain. If you don't run a full node, you outsource verification of Bitcoin blocks to someone else and trust them to tell you the truth, which means you're not using Bitcoin trustlessly.

David Harding has authored an article on the bitcoin.org website explaining how running a full node - or using Bitcoin trustlessly - actually helps you.

The bitcoin currency only works when people accept bitcoins in exchange for other valuable things. That means it's the people accepting bitcoins who give it value and who get to decide how Bitcoin should work.

When you accept bitcoins, you have the power to enforce Bitcoin's rules, such as preventing confiscation of any person's bitcoins without access to that person's private keys.

*Unfortunately, **many users outsource their enforcement power**. This leaves Bitcoin's decentralization in a weakened state where a handful of miners can collude with a handful of banks and free services to change Bitcoin's rules for all those non-verifying users who outsourced their power.*

*Unlike other wallets, **Bitcoin Core does enforce the rules**—so if the miners and banks change the rules for their non-verifying users, those users will be unable to pay full validation Bitcoin Core users like you.*

— David Harding on Full Validation – bitcoin.org (2015)

He says that running a full node will help you verify every aspect of the blockchain without trusting anyone else, so as to ensure that the coins you receive from others are genuine. This is great, but there's one important thing that a full node can't help you with: it can't prevent double- spending through chain rewrites:

> Note that although all programs—including Bitcoin Core—are vulnerable to chain rewrites, Bitcoin provides a defense mechanism: the more confirmations your transactions have, the safer you are. There is no known decentralized defense better than that.
>
> — David Harding on Full Validation – bitcoin.org (2015)

No matter how advanced your software is, you still have to trust that the blocks containing your coins won't be rewritten. However, as pointed out by Harding, you can await a number of confirmations, after which you consider the probability of a chain rewrite small enough to be acceptable.

The incentives for using Bitcoin in a trustless way align with the system's need for full node decentralization. The more people who use their own full nodes, the more full node decentralization, and thus the stronger Bitcoin stands against malicious changes to the protocol. But unfortunately, as explained in the full node decentralization section, users often opt for trusted services as consequence of the inevitable trade-off between trustlessness and convenience.

Bitcoin's trustlessness is absolutely imperative from a system perspective. In 2018, Matt Corallo, spoke about trustlessness at the Baltic Honeybadger conference in Riga. The essence of that talk is that you can't build trustless systems on top of a trusted system, but you can build trusted systems - for example, a custodial wallet - on top of a trustless system.

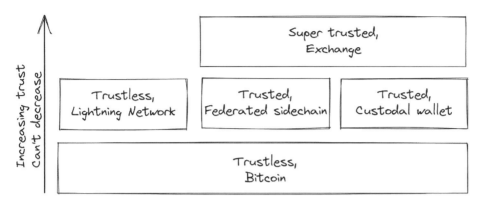

Figure 2.1: A trustless base layer allows for various trade-offs on higher levels.

This security model allows the system designer to select trade-offs that make sense to them without forcing those trade-offs on others.

Don't trust, verify

Bitcoin works trustlessly, but you still have to trust your software and hardware to some degree. That's because your software or hardware might not be programmed to do what's stated on the box. For example:

- The CPU might be maliciously designed to detect private key cryptographic operations and leak the private key data.

- The operating system's random number generator might not be as random as it claims.

- Bitcoin Core might have sneaked in code that will send your private keys to some bad actor.

So, besides running a full node, you also need to make sure you're running what you intend to. Reddit user brianddk wrote an article about the various levels of trust you can choose from, when verifying your software. In the section "Trusting the builders", he talks about *reproducible builds*:

> *Reproducible builds are a way to design software so that many community developers can each build the software and ensure that the final installer built is identical to what other developers produce. With a very public, reproducible project like bitcoin, no single developer needs to be completely trusted. Many developers can all perform the build and attest that they produced the same file as the one the original builder digitally signed.*
>
> *— brianddk on Reddit Bitcoin v22.0 and Guix; Stronger defense against the "Trusting Trust Attack" (2022)*

The article defines 5 levels of trust: trusting the site, the builders, the compiler, the kernel, and the hardware.

To further deepen the topic of reproducible builds, Carl Dong made a presentation about Guix explaining why trusting the operating system, libraries, and compilers can be problematic, and how to fix that with a system called Guix, which is used by Bitcoin Core today.

> *So what can we do about the fact that our toolchain can have a bunch of trusted binaries that can be reproducibly malicious? We need to be more than reproducible. We need to be bootstrappable. We cannot have that many binary tools that we need to download and trust from external servers controlled by other organizations. We should know how these tools are built and exactly how we can go through the process of building them again, preferably from a much smaller set of trusted binaries. We need to minimize our trusted set of binaries as much as possible, and have an easily auditable path from those toolchains to what we use how to build bitcoin. This allows us to maximize verification and minimize trust.*
>
> *— Carl Dong on Guix – Breaking Bitcoin Conference (2019)*

He then explains how Guix allows us to only trust a minimal binary of 357 bytes that can be verified and fully understood if you know how to interpret the instructions. This is quite remarkable: one verifies that the 357-byte binary does what it should, then uses it to build the full build system from source code, and ends up with a Bitcoin Core binary that should be an exact copy of anyone else's build.

There's a mantra that many bitcoiners subscribe to, which captures well much of the above:

> *Don't trust, verify.*
>
> — *Bitcoiners everywhere*

This alludes to the phrase "trust, but verify" that former U.S. president Ronald Reagan used in the context of nuclear disarmament. Bitcoiners switched it around to highlight the rejection of trust and the importance of running a full node.

It's up to the users to decide to what degree they want to verify the software they use and the blockchain data they receive. As with so many other things in Bitcoin, there's a trade-off between convenience and trustlessness. It's almost always more convenient to use a custodial wallet compared to running Bitcoin Core on your own hardware. However, as Bitcoin software is maturing and user interfaces are improving, over time it should get better at supporting users willing to work towards trustlessness. Also, as users gain more knowledge over time, they should be able to gradually remove trust from the equation.

Some users think adversarially (see Adversarial thinking) and verify most aspects of the software they run. As a consequence, they reduce the need for trust to the bare minimum, as they only need to trust their computer hardware and operating system. In doing so, they also help people who don't verify their hardware as thoroughly by raising their voices in public to warn about any issues they might find. One good example of this is an event that occurred in 2018, when someone discovered a bug that would allow miners to spend an output twice in the same transaction:

CVE-2018-17144, a fix for which was released on September 18th in Bitcoin Core versions 0.16.3 and 0.17.0rc4, includes both a Denial of Service component and a critical inflation vulnerability. It was originally reported to several developers working on Bitcoin Core, as well as projects supporting other cryptocurrencies, including ABC and Unlimited on September 17th as a Denial of Service bug only, however we quickly determined that the issue was also an inflation vulnerability with the same root cause and fix.

— *CVE-2018-17144 Full Disclosure on bitcoincore.org (2018)*

Here, an anonymous person reported an issue that turned out much worse than the reporter realized. This highlights the fact that people who verify the code often report security flaws instead of exploiting them. This is beneficial to those who aren't able to verify everything themselves. However, users should not trust others to keep them safe, but should rather verify for themselves whenever and whatever they can; that's how one remains as sovereign as possible, and how Bitcoin prospers. The more eyes on the software, the less likely it is that malicious code and security flaws slip through.

Conclusion

The Bitcoin protocol is trustless because it allows users to interact with it without trusting a third party. In practice, however, most people aren't able to verify the full stack of software and hardware they run Bitcoin on. Skilled people that verify software or hardware are able to warn other, less skilled, people when they find malicious code or bugs.

Without trustlessness, we can't have decentralizaion, because trust inevitebly involves some central point of authority. You can build a trusted system on top of a trustless system, but you can't build a trustless system on top of a trusted system.

3

PRIVACY

This chapter deals with how to keep your private financial information to yourself. It explains what privacy stands for in the context of Bitcoin, why it's important, and what it means to say that Bitcoin is pseudonymous. It also looks into how private data can leak, both on-chain and off-chain. Then, it talks about the fact that bitcoins should be fungible, meaning interchangeable for any other bitcoins, and how fungibility and privacy go hand in hand. Lastly, the chapter introduces some measures you can take to improve your privacy and that of others.

Bitcoin can be described as a pseudonymous system (see Pseudonymity for further details on this), where users have multiple pseudonyms in the form of public keys. At first glance, this looks like a pretty good way to protect users from being identified, but it is in fact really easy to leak private financial information unintentionally.

What does privacy mean?

Privacy can mean different things in different contexts. In Bitcoin, it generally means that users don't have to reveal their financial information to others, unless they voluntarily do so.

There are many ways in which you may leak your private information to others, with or without knowing it. Data can either leak from the public blockchain or through other means, for example when malicious actors intercept your internet communications.

Why is privacy important?

It may seem obvious why privacy is important in Bitcoin, but there are some aspects of it that one might not immediately think about. On the Bitcoin Talk forum, Gregory Maxwell walks us through a lot of good reasons why he thinks privacy matters. Among them are free market, safety, and human dignity:

> *Financial privacy is an essential criteria for the efficient operation of a free market: if you run a business, you cannot effectively set prices if your suppliers and customers can see all your transactions against your will. You cannot compete effectively if your competition is tracking your sales. Individually your informational leverage is lost in your private dealings if you don't have privacy over your accounts: if you pay your landlord in Bitcoin without enough privacy in place, your landlord will see when you've received a pay raise and can hit you up for more rent.*
>
> *Financial privacy is essential for personal safety: if thieves can see your spending, income, and holdings, they can use that information to target and exploit you.*

Without privacy malicious parties have more ability to steal your identity, snatch your large purchases off your doorstep, or impersonate businesses you transact with towards you... they can tell exactly how much to try to scam you for.

Financial privacy is essential for human dignity: no one wants the snotty barista at the coffee shop or their nosy neighbors commenting on their income or spending habits. No one wants their baby-crazy in-laws asking why they're buying contraception (or sex toys). Your employer has no business knowing what church you donate to. Only in a perfectly enlightened discrimination free world where no one has undue authority over anyone else could we retain our dignity and make our lawful transactions freely without self-censorship if we don't have privacy.

— *Gregory Maxwell – Bitcoin Talk forum (2013)*

Maxwell also touches on fungibility, which will be discussed later in this chapter, as well as on how privacy and law enforcement are not contradictory.

Pseudonymity

We mentioned above that Bitcoin is pseudonymous, and that the pseudonyms are public keys. In the media you often hear that Bitcoin is anonymous, which is not correct. There is a distinction between anonymity and pseudonymity.

Andrew Poelstra explains in a Bitcoin Stack Exchange post what anonymity would look like in transactions:

Total anonymity, in the sense that when you spend money there is no trace of where it came from or where it's going, is theoretically possible by using the cryptographic technique of zero-knowledge proofs.

— *Andrew Poelstra on anonymity – Bitcoin Stack Exchange (2016)*

The difference seems to be that in a pseudonymous form of money you can trace payments between pseudonyms, whereas in an anonymous form of money you can't. Since bitcoin payments are traceable between pseudonyms, it's not an anonymous system.

We have also said that the pseudonyms are public keys, but it's actually addresses derived from public keys. Why do we use addresses as pseudonyms and not something else, for example some descriptive names, like "watchme1984"? This has been explained well by user Tim S., also on Bitcoin Stack Exchange:

> In order for Bitcoin's idea to work, you must have coins that can only be spent by the owner of a given private key. This means that whatever you send to must be tied, in some way, to a public key.
>
> Using arbitrary pseudonyms (e.g. user names) would mean that you'd have to then somehow link the pseudonym to a public key in order to enable public/private key crypto. This would remove the ability to securely create addresses/pseudonyms offline (e.g. before someone could send money to the user name "tdumidu", you'd have to announce in the blockchain that "tdumidu" is owned by public key "a1c... ", and include a fee so others have a reason to announce it), reduce anonymity (by encouraging you to reuse pseudonyms), and needlessly bloat the size of the blockchain. It would also create a false sense of security that you're sending to who you think you are (if I take the name "Linus Torvalds" before he does, then it's mine and people might send money thinking they're paying the creator of Linux, not me).
>
> — Tim S. on pseudonyms – Bitcoin Stack Exchange (2014)

By using addresses, or public keys, we achieve important goals, such as removing the need to somehow register a pseudonym beforehand, reducing the incentives for pseudonym reuse, avoiding blockchain bloat, and making it harder to impersonate other people.

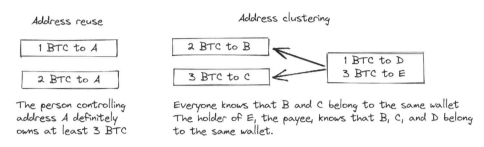

Figure 3.1: Typical privacy leaks on the blockchain.

Blockchain privacy

Blockchain privacy refers to the information you disclose by transacting on the blockchain. It applies to all transactions, the ones you send as well as the ones you receive.

Satoshi Nakamoto ponders over on-chain privacy in section 7 of his Bitcoin whitepaper:

> *As an additional firewall, a new key pair should be used for each transaction to keep them from being linked to a common owner. Some linking is still unavoidable with multi-input transactions, which necessarily reveal that their inputs were owned by the same owner. The risk is that if the owner of a key is revealed, linking could reveal other transactions that belonged to the same owner.*
>
> *— Satoshi Nakamoto – Bitcoin: A Peer-to-Peer Electronic Cash System (2008)*

The paper summarizes the main problems of blockchain privacy, namely address reuse and address clustering. The first is self-explaining, the latter refers to the ability to decide, with some level of certainty, that a set of different addresses belongs to the same user.

Chris Belcher wrote in great detail about the different kinds of privacy leaks that can happen on the Bitcoin blockchain. We recommend you read at least the first few subsections under "Blockchain attacks on privacy."

The takeaway is that privacy in Bitcoin isn't perfect. It requires a significant amount of work to transact privately. Most people aren't prepared to go that far for privacy. There seems to be a clear trade-off between privacy and usability.

Another important aspect of privacy is that the measures you take to protect your own privacy affect other users as well. If you are sloppy with your own privacy, other people might experience reduced privacy, too. Gregory Maxwell explains this very plainly on the same Bitcoin Talk discussion that we linked above, and concludes with an example:

> *This actually works in practice, too... A nice whitehat hacker on IRC was playing around with brainwallet cracking and hit a phrase with ~250 BTC in it. We were able to identify the owner from just the address alone, because they'd been paid by a Bitcoin service that reused addresses and he was able to talk them into giving up the users contact information. He actually got the user on the phone, they were shocked and confused— but grateful to not be out their coin. A happy ending there. (This isn't the only example of it, by far ... but its one of the more fun ones).*

> *— Gregory Maxwell – Bitcoin Talk forum (2013)*

In this case, it all went well thanks to the philanthropically-minded hacker, but don't count on that next time.

Non-blockchain privacy

While the blockchain proves to be a notorious source of privacy leaks, there are plenty of other leaks that don't use the blockchain, some sneakier than others. These range from key-loggers to network traffic analysis. To read up on some of these methods, please refer again to Chris Belcher's piece, specifically the section "Non-blockchain attacks on privacy".

Among a plethora of attacks, Belcher mentions the possibility of someone snooping on your internet connection, for example, your ISP:

> *If the adversary sees a transaction or block coming out of your node which did not previously enter, then it can know with near-certainty that the transaction was made by you or the block was mined by you. As internet connections are involved, the adversary will be able to link the IP address with the discovered bitcoin information.*
>
> — *Chris Belcher – Bitcoin wiki*

However, among the most obvious privacy leaks are exchanges. Due to laws, usually referred to as KYC (Know Your Customer) and AML (Anti-Money Laundering), that are valid in the jurisdictions they operate in, exchanges and related companies often have to collect personal data about their users, building up big databases about which users own which bitcoins. These databases are great honeypots for evil governments and criminals who are always on the lookout for new victims. There are actual markets for this kind of data, where hackers sell data to the highest bidder. To make things worse, the companies that manage these databases often have little experience with protecting financial data, in fact many of them are young start-ups, and we know for a fact that several leaks have already occurred. A few examples are India-based MobiQwik and HubSpot

Again, protecting data against this wide range of attacks is hard, and it is likely that you won't be fully able to do so. You'll have to opt for the trade-off between convenience and privacy that works best for you.

Fungibility

Fungibility, in the context of currencies, means that one coin is interchangeable for any other coin of the same currency. This funny word was briefly touched upon in Why is privacy important?. In the article discussed there, Gregory Maxwell stated

> *Financial privacy is an essential element to fungibility in Bitcoin: if you can meaningfully distinguish one coin from another, then their fungibility is weak. If our fungibility is too weak in practice, then we cannot be decentralized: if someone important announces a list of stolen coins they won't accept coins derived from, you must carefully check coins you accept against that list and return the ones that fail. Everyone gets stuck checking blacklists issued by various authorities because in that world we'd all not like to get stuck with bad coins. This adds friction and transactional costs and makes Bitcoin less valuable as a money.*
>
> *— Gregory Maxwell – Bitcoin Talk forum (2013)*

Here, he speaks about the dangers derived from a lack of fungibility. Suppose that you have a UTXO. That UTXO's history can normally be traced back several hops, fanning out to multitudes of previous outputs. If any of those outputs were involved in any illegal, unwanted, or suspicious activity, then some potential recipients of your coin might reject it. If you think

that your payees will verify your coins against some centralized whitelist
or blacklist service, you might start checking the coins you receive too, just
to be on the safe side. The result is that bad fungibility will bolster even
worse fungibility.

Adam Back and Matt Corallo gave a presentation about fungibility at Scaling Bitcoin in Milan in 2016. They were thinking along the same lines:

> *You need fungibility for bitcoin to function. If you receive coins and can't spend*
> *them, then you start to doubt whether you can spend them. If there are doubts*
> *about coins you receive, then people are going to go to taint services and check*
> *whether "are these coins blessed" and then people are going to refuse to trade. What*
> *this does is it transitions bitcoin from a decentralized permissionless system into*
> *a centralized permissioned system where you have an "IOU" from the blacklist*
> *providers.*
>
> — *Matt Corallo and Adam Back – Fungibility Overview (2016)*

It seems that privacy and fungibility go hand-in-hand. Fungibility will
weaken if privacy is weak, for example as coins from unwanted people may
become blacklisted. In the same way, privacy will weaken if fungibility
is weak: if there is a blacklist, you will have to ask the blacklist providers
about which coins to accept, thereby possibly revealing your IP address,
email address, and other sensitive information. These two features are so
intertwined that it's hard to talk about either of them in isolation.

Privacy measures

Several techniques have been developed to help people protecting themselves from privacy leaks. Among the most obvious ones is, as noted by
Nakamoto in section Blockchain privacy above, using unique addresses

for every transaction, but several others exist. We're not going to teach you how to become a privacy ninja. However, Bitcoin Q+A has a quick summary of privacy-enhancing technologies, somewhat ordered by how hard they are to implement. When you read it, you'll notice that Bitcoin privacy often has to do with stuff outside of Bitcoin. For example, you shouldn't brag about your bitcoins, and you should use Tor and VPN. The post also lists some measures directly related to Bitcoin:

Full node If you don't use your own full node, you will leak lots of information about your wallet to servers on the internet. Running a full node is a great first step.

Lightning Network Several protocols exist on top of Bitcoin, for example the Lightning Network and Blockstream's Liquid sidechain.

CoinJoin A way for multiple people to merge their transactions into one, making it harder to do chain analysis.

In a talk at the Breaking Bitcoin conference, Chris Belcher gave an interesting practical example of how privacy has been improved.

> *They were a bitcoin casino. Online gambling is not allowed in the US. Any customers of Coinbase that deposited straight to Bustabit would have their accounts shutdown because Coinbase was monitoring for this. Bustabit did a few things. They did something called change avoidance where you go through– and you see if you can construct a transaction that has no change output. This saves miner fees and also hinders analysis. Also, they imported their heavily-used reused deposit addresses into joinmarket. At this point, coinbase.com customers never got banned. It seems Coinbase's surveillance service was unable to do the analysis after this, so it is possible to break these algorithms.*
>
> *— Chris Belcher in "Breaking Bitcoin Privacy" Breaking Bitcoin conference (2019)*

He also mentioned this example, among others, on the Privacy page on the Bitcoin wiki.

Note how better privacy can be achieved by building systems on top of Bitcoin, as is the case with Lightning Network:

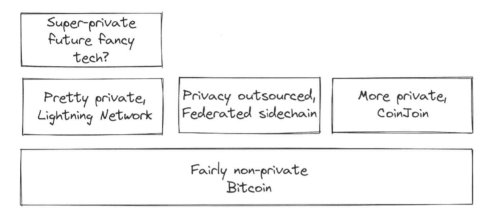

Figure 3.2: Layers on top of Bitcoin can add privacy.

We noted in Trustlessness that the need for trust can only increase with layers on top, but that doesn't seem to be the case for privacy, which can be improved or made worse arbitrarily in layers on top. Why is that? Any layer on top of Bitcoin, as explained in Layered scaling, must use on-chain transactions occasionally, otherwise it wouldn't be "on top of Bitcoin". Privacy-enhancing layers generally try to use the base layer as little as possible to minimize the amount of information revealed.

The above are somewhat technical ways to improve your privacy. But there are other ways. At the beginning of this chapter, we said that Bitcoin is a pseudonymous system. This means that users in Bitcoin aren't known by their real names or other personal data, but by their public keys. A public key is a pseudonym for a user, and a user can have multiple pseudonyms. In an ideal world, your in-person identity is decoupled from your Bitcoin pseudonyms. Unfortunately, due to the privacy problems described in this chapter, this decoupling usually degrades over time.

To mitigate the risks of having your personal data revealed is to not give it out in the first place nor to give it to centralized services, which build big databases that can leak (see Non-blockchain privacy). An article by Bitcoin Q+A explains KYC and the dangers derived from it. It also suggests some steps you can take to improve your situation.

> *Thankfully there are some options out there to purchase Bitcoin via no KYC sources. These are all P2P (peer to peer) exchanges where you are trading directly with another individual and not a centralised third party. Unfortunately some sell other coins as well as bitcoin so we urge you to take care.*
>
> *— Bitcoin Q+A, noKYC only, Avoid the creep – bitcoiner.guide*

The article suggests you avoid using exchanges that require KYC/AML and instead trade in private, or use decentralized exchanges like bisq.

For more in-depth reading about countermeasures, refer to the previously mentioned wiki article on privacy, starting at "Methods for improving privacy (non-blockchain)".

Conclusion

Privacy is very important but hard to achieve. There is no privacy silver bullet. To get decent privacy in Bitcoin, you have to take active measures, some of which are costly and time-consuming.

4

Finite supply

This chapter looks into the bitcoin supply limit of 21 million BTC, or how much is it actually? We talk about how this limit is enforced and what one can do to verify that it's being respected. Moreover, we take a peek into the crystal ball and discuss the dynamics that will come into play when the block reward shifts from subsidy-based to fee-based.

The well-known finite supply of 21 million BTC is regarded as a fundamental property of Bitcoin. But is it really set in stone?

Let's start by looking at what the current consensus rules say about the supply of bitcoin, and how much of it will actually be usable. Pieter Wuille wrote a piece about this on Stack Exchange, in which he counted how many bitcoins there would be once all coins are mined:

*If you sum all these numbers together, you get **20999999.9769** BTC.*

— Pieter Wuille – Stack Exchange (2015)

But due to a number of reasons — such as early problems with coinbase transactions, miners who unintentionally claim less than allowed, and loss of private keys — that upper limit will never be reached. Wuille concludes:

*This leaves us with **20999817.31308491** BTC (taking everything up to block 528333 into account)*

... However, various wallets have been lost or stolen, transactions have been sent to the wrong address, people forgot they owned bitcoin. The totals of this may well be millions. People have tried to tally known losses up here.

*This leaves us with: **???** BTC.*

— Pieter Wuille – Stack Exchange (2015)

We can thus be sure that the bitcoin supply will be 20999817.31308491 BTC at most. Any lost or unverifiably burnt coins will make this number lower, but we don't know by how much. The interesting thing is that it doesn't really matter, or better yet it does matter in a positive way for bitcoin holders, as explained by Satoshi Nakamoto:

Lost coins only make everyone else's coins worth slightly more. Think of it as a donation to everyone.

— Satoshi Nakamoto on lost bitcoins – Bitcointalk forum (2010)

The finite supply will shrink and this should, at least in theory, cause price deflation.

More important than the exact number of coins in circulation is the way the supply limit is enforced without any central authority. Alias chytrik puts it well on Stack Exchange.

> *So the answer is that you don't have to trust someone to not increase the supply. You just have to run some code that will verify that they haven't.*
>
> — *chytrik – Stack Exchange (2021)*

Even if some full nodes turn to the dark side and decide to accept blocks with higher-value coinbase transactions, all the remaining full nodes will simply neglect them and continue doing business as usual. Some full nodes may, intentionally or unintentionally (see 2010-08-15 Combined output overflow (CVE-2010-5139)), run evil softwares, yet the collective will robustly secure the blockchain. In conclusion, you can choose to trust the system without having to trust anyone.

Block subsidy and transaction fees

A block reward is composed of the block subsidy plus transaction fees. The block reward needs to cover Bitcoin's security costs. We can say for sure that under today's conditions with regard to block subsidy, transaction fees, bitcoin price, mempool size, hash power, degree of decentralization etc., the incentives for every player to play by the rules are high enough to preserve a secure monetary system.

What happens when the block subsidy approaches zero? To keep things simple, let's assume it actually equals zero. At this point, the system's security cost is covered through transaction fees only. What the future holds for us when this happens, we cannot know. The uncertainty factors are numerous and we are left to speculations. For example, Paul Sztorc's contribution to the subject in his Truthcoin blog is mostly speculations, but he has at least one solid point (please note that M2, as referred to by Sztorc, is a measurement of a fiat money supply):

> While the two are mixed into the same "security budget", the block subsidy and txn-fees are utterly and completely different. They are as different from each other, as "VISA's total profits in 2017" are from the "total increase in M2 in 2017".
> — Paul Sztorc on Security Budget in the Long Run – Truthcoin blog (2019)

Today, it is holders who pay for security (via monetary inflation). Tomorrow it will be the spenders' turn to somehow shoulder this burden, as illustrated in Figure 4.1.

When transaction fees are the main motivation for mining, the incentives shift. Most notably, if the mempool of a miner doesn't contain enough transaction fees, it might become more profitable for that miner to rewrite Bitcoin's history rather than extending it. Bitcoin Optech has a specific section on this behavior, called *fee sniping*, written by David Harding:

> Fee sniping is a problem that may occur as Bitcoin's subsidy continues to diminish and transaction fees begin to dominate Bitcoin's block rewards. If transaction fees are all that matter, then a miner with x percent of the hash rate has a x percent chance of mining the next block, so the expected value to them of honestly mining is x percent of the best feerate set of transactions in their mempool.
>
> Alternatively, a miner could dishonestly attempt to re-mine the previous block plus a wholly new block to extend the chain. This behavior is referred to as fee sniping, and the dishonest miner's chance of succeeding at it if every other miner is honest is $(x/(1-x))^2$. Even though fee sniping has an overall lower probability of success than honest mining, attempting dishonest mining could be the more

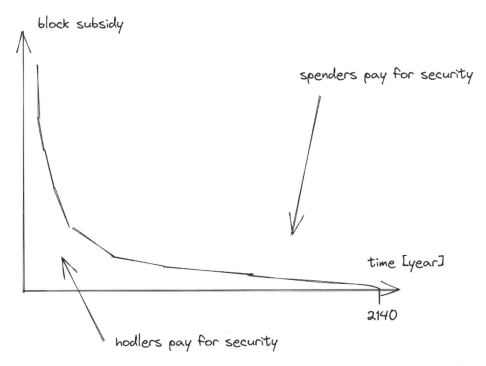

Figure 4.1: As time goes by, the bearing of security costs will shift from holders to spenders.

profitable choice if transactions in the previous block paid significantly higher feerates than the transactions currently in the mempool—a small chance at a large amount can be worth more than a large chance at a small amount.

— David Harding, fee sniping Bitcoin Optech website

Throwing a wet blanket over our hopes for the future is the fact that if miners start conducting fee sniping, this will incentivize others to do the same, leaving even fewer honest miners. This could severely impair the overall security of Bitcoin. Harding goes on to list a few countermeasures that can be taken, such as relying on transaction time locks to restrict where in the blockchain the transaction may appear.

So, given that the consensus on finite supply remains, the block subsidy will - thanks to BIP42 which fixed a very-long-term inflation bug - get to zero around year 2140. Will the transaction fees thereafter be enough to secure the network? It's impossible to say, but we do know a few things:

- A century is a *long* time from the Bitcoin perspective. If it is still around, it will have probably evolved enormously.

- If an overwhelming economic majority finds it necessary to change the rules and introduce for example a perpetual annual 0.1% or 1% monetary inflation, the supply of bitcoin will no longer be finite.

- With zero block subsidy and an empty or nearly empty mempool, things can become shaky due to fee sniping.

Since the transition to a fee-only block reward is so far in the future, it might be wise not to jump to conclusions and try to fix the potential issues while we can. For example, Peter Todd thinks there's an actual risk that Bitcoin's security budget won't be enough in the future, and consequently argues for a small perpetual inflation in Bitcoin. However, he also thinks it's not a good idea to discuss such an issue at this time, as

he said on the What Bitcoin Did podcast:

> But, that's a risk like 10, 20 years in the future. That is a very long time. And, by then, who the hell knows what the risks are?
> — Peter Todd on security budget – What Bitcoin Did podcast (2019)

Perhaps we could think of Bitcoin as something organic. Imagine a small, slowly-growing oak plant. Imagine also that you have never seen a fully grown tree in your life. Wouldn't it be wise then to restrain your control issues instead of setting in advance all the rules on how this plant should be allowed to evolve and grow?

Conclusion

Whether the bitcoin supply will grow past 21 million we cannot say today, and that is probably not so bad. Ensuring that the security budget remains high enough is crucial but not urgent. Let's have this discussion in 10-50 years, when we know more. If it's still relevant.

5

Upgrading

Upgrading Bitcoin in a safe way can be extremely difficult. Some changes take several years to roll out. In this chapter, we learn about the common vocabulary around upgrading Bitcoin, and explore some examples of historic upgrades to its protocol as well as the insights that we gained from them. Finally, we talk about chain splits and the risks and costs related to them.

To get in tune for this chapter, you should read David Harding's piece on harmony and discord.

> *Bitcoin experts talk often of consensus, whose meaning is abstract and hard to pin down. But the word consensus evolved from the Latin word concentus, "a singing together, harmony,"[1] so let us talk not of Bitcoin consensus but of Bitcoin harmony.*

Harmony is what makes Bitcoin work. Thousands of full nodes each work independently to verify the transactions they receive are valid, producing a harmonious agreement about the state of the Bitcoin ledger without any node operator needing to trust anyone else. It's similar to a chorus where each member sings the same song at the same time to produce something far more beautiful than any of them could produce alone.

The result of Bitcoin harmony is a system where bitcoins are safe not just from petty thieves (provided you keep your keys secure) but also from endless inflation, mass or targeted confiscation, or simply the bureaucratic morass that is the legacy financial system.

— David Harding – Harmony and Discord

This chapter discusses how Bitcoin can be upgraded without causing discord. Staying in harmony, i.e. maintaining consensus, is indeed one of the biggest challenges in Bitcoin development. There are lots of nuances to upgrade mechanisms, which might be best understood by studying actual cases of previous upgrades. For this reason, the chapter puts much focus on historic examples, and it starts by setting the stage with some useful vocabulary.

Vocabulary

According to Wikipedia, forward compatibility refers to the condition in which an old software can process data created by newer softwares, ignoring the parts it doesn't understand.

A standard supports forward compatibility if a product that complies with earlier versions can "gracefully" process input designed for later versions of the standard, ignoring new parts which it does not understand.

— Forward compatibility Wikipedia

Vice versa, backward compatibility refers to when data from an old software is usable on newer softwares. A change is said to be fully compatible if it's both forward and backward compatible.

A change to the Bitcoin consensus rules is said to be a **soft fork** if it is fully compatible. This is the most common way to upgrade Bitcoin, for a number of reasons that we'll discuss further in this chapter. If a change to the Bitcoin consensus rules is backward compatible but not forward compatible, it is called a **hard fork**.

For a technical overview of soft forks and hard forks, please read chapter 11 of Grokking Bitcoin. It explains these terms and also dives into the upgrade mechanisms. It's recommended, although not strictly necessary, to get a grip on this before you continue reading.

Historic upgrades

Bitcoin is not the same today as it was when the genesis block was created. Several upgrades have been made throughout the years. In 2017, Eric Lombrozo spoke at the Breaking Bitcoin conference about Bitcoin's different upgrading mechanisms, pointing out how much they have evolved over time. He even explained how Satoshi Nakamoto once upgraded Bitcoin through a hard fork.

> *There was actually a hard-fork in bitcoin that Satoshi did that we would never do it this way- it's a pretty bad way to do it. If you look at the git commit description here [757f076], he says something about reverted makefile.unix wx-config version 0.3.6. Right. That's all it says. It has no indication that it has a breaking change at all. He was basically hiding it in there. He also posted to bitcointalk and said, please*

upgrade to 0.3.6 ASAP. We fixed an implementation bug where it is possible that bogus transactions can be displayed as accepted. Do not accept bitcoin payments until you upgrade to 0.3.6. If you can't upgrade right away, then it would be best to shutdown your bitcoin node until you do. And then on top of that, I don't know why he decided to do this as well, he decided to add some optimizations in the same code. Fix a bug and add some optimizations.

— Eric Lombrozo – Changing Consensus Rules Without Breaking Bitcoin at Breaking Bitcoin conference (2017)

He points out that, be it intentionally or not, this hard fork created opportunities for future soft forks, namely the Script operators (opcodes) OP_NOP1-OP_NOP10. We'll look more into this code change in 2010-07-28: Spend anyone's coins (CVE-2010-5141). These opcodes have been used for two soft forks so far: BIP65 (OP_CHECKLOCKTIMEVERIFY), and BIP113 (OP_SEQUENCEVERIFY).

Lombrozo also provides an overview of the way upgrade mechanisms have evolved throughout the years, up until 2017. Since then, only one other major upgrade, Taproot (analyzed in Taproot upgrade - Speedy Trial), has been deployed. The long and somewhat chaotic process that led to its activation has helped us gain further insights on upgrading mechanisms in Bitcoin.

Segwit upgrade

While all the upgrades preceding Segwit had been more or less painless, this one was different. When Segwit activation code was released, in October 2016, there seemed to be overwhelming support for it among Bitcoin users, but for some reason miners didn't signal support for this upgrade, which stalled the activation with no resolution in sight.

Aaron van Wirdum describes this winding road in his Bitcoin Magazine article The Long Road To Segwit. He starts by explaining what Segwit is and how that taps into the block size debate. Van Wirdum then outlines the turn of events that led to its final activation. At the center of this process was an upgrade mechanism called *user activated soft fork*, or UASF for short, that was proposed by user Shaolinfry.

> *Shaolinfry proposed an alternative: a user activated soft fork (UASF). Instead of hash power activation, a user activated soft fork would have a "'flag day activation' where nodes begin enforcement at a predetermined time in the future." As long as such a UASF is enforced by an economic majority, this should compel a majority of miners to follow (or activate) the soft fork.*
>
> — *Aaron van Wirdum – The Long Road To Segwit on Bitcoin Magazine (2017)*

Among other things, he cites Shaolinfry's email to the Bitcoin-dev mailing list. In that occasion Shaolinfry argued against miner activated soft forks, listing a number of problems with them.

> *Firstly, it requires trusting the hash power will validate after activation. The BIP66 soft fork was a case where 95% of the hashrate was signaling readiness but in reality about half was not actually validating the upgraded rules and mined upon an invalid block by mistake[1].*
>
> *Secondly, miner signalling has a natural veto which allows a small percentage of hashrate to veto node activation of the upgrade for everyone. To date, soft forks have taken advantage of the relatively centralised mining landscape where there are relatively few mining pools building valid blocks; as we move towards more hashrate decentralization, it's likely that we will suffer more and more from "upgrade inertia" which will veto most upgrades.*
>
> — *Shaolinfry – Bitcoin-dev mailing list (2017)*

Shaolinfry also drew attention to a common misinterpretation of miner signaling: people generally thought that it was a means by which miners could decide upon protocol upgrades, rather than an action that helped coordinate upgrades. Due to this misunderstanding, miners might have also felt obliged to proclaim in public their views on a certain soft fork, as if that gave weight to the proposal.

The UASF proposal is, in a nutshell, a "flag day" on which nodes start enforcing specific new rules. That way, miners don't have to make a collective effort to coordinate the upgrade, but *can* trigger activation earlier than the flag day if enough blocks signal support.

> *My suggestion is to have the best of both worlds. Since a user activated soft fork needs a relatively long lead time before activation, we can combine with BIP9 to give the option of a faster hash power coordinated activation or activation by flag day, whichever is the sooner. In both cases, we can leverage the warning systems in BIP9. The change is relatively simple, adding an activation-time parameter which will transition the BIP9 state to LOCKED_IN before the end of the BIP9 deployment timeout.*
>
> *— Shaolinfry – Bitcoin-dev mailing list (2017)*

 This idea caught a lot of interest, but didn't seem to reach near unanimous support, which caused concern for a potential chain split. The article by Aaron van Wirdum explains how this finally got resolved thanks to BIP91, authored by James Hilliard.

> *Hilliard proposed a slightly complex but clever solution that would make every- thing compatible: Segregated Witness activation as proposed by the Bitcoin Core development team, the BIP148 UASF and the New York Agreement activation mechanism. His BIP91 could keep Bitcoin whole — at least throughout SegWit activation.*
>
> *— Aaron van Wirdum – The Long Road To Segwit on Bitcoin Magazine (2017)*

There were some more complicating factors involved (e.g. the so-called "New York Agreement"), that this BIP had to take into consideration. We encourage you to read Van Wirdum's article in full to learn about the many interesting details in this story.

Post-Segwit discussion

After the Segwit deployment, a discussion about deployment mechanisms emerged. As noted by Eric Lombrozo in his talk at the Breaking Bitcoin conference and by Shaolinfry (see Segwit upgrade above), a miner activated soft fork isn't the ideal upgrade mechanism.

> *At some point we're probably going to want to add more features to the bitcoin protocol. This is a big philosophical question we're asking ourselves. Do we do a UASF for the next one? What about a hybrid approach? Miner activated by itself has been ruled out. bip9 we're not going to use again.*
>
> *— Eric Lombrozo – Changing Consensus Rules Without Breaking Bitcoin at Breaking Bitcoin conference (2017)*

In January 2020, Matt Corallo sent an email to the Bitcoin-dev mailing list that started a discussion on future soft fork deployment mechanisms. He listed five goals that he thought were essential in an upgrade. David Harding summarizes them in a Bitcoin Optech newsletter as:

1. *The ability to abort if a serious objection to the proposed consensus rules changes is encountered*

2. *The allocation of enough time after the release of updated software to ensure that most economic nodes are upgraded to enforce those rules*

3. *The expectation that the network hash rate will be roughly the same before and after the change, as well as during any transition*

4. *The prevention, as much as possible, of the creation of blocks that are invalid under the new rules, which could lead to false confirmations in non-upgraded nodes and SPV clients*

5. *The assurance that the abort mechanisms can't be misused by griefers or partisans to withhold a widely desired upgrade with no known problems*

— David Harding – Bitcoin Optech newsletter #80 (2020)

What Corallo proposes is a combination of a miner activated soft fork and a user activated soft fork:

Thus, as something a bit more concrete, I think an activation method which sets the right precedent and appropriately considers the above goals, would be:

1) a standard BIP 9 deployment with a one-year time horizon for activation with 95% miner readiness,
2) in the case that no activation occurs within a year, a six month quieting period during which the community can analyze and discussion the reasons for no activation and,
3) in the case that it makes sense, a simple command-line/bitcoin.conf parameter which was supported since the original deployment release would enable users to opt into a BIP 8 deployment with a 24-month time-horizon for flag-day activation (as well as a new Bitcoin Core release enabling the flag universally).

This provides a very long time horizon for more standard activation, while still ensuring the goals in #5 are met, even if, in those cases, the time horizon needs to be significantly extended to meet the goals of #3. Developing Bitcoin is not a race. If we have to, waiting 42 months ensures we're not setting a negative precedent that we'll come to regret as Bitcoin continues to grow.

— Matt Corallo – Modern Soft Fork Activation on Bitcoin-dev mailing list (2020)

Taproot upgrade - Speedy Trial

When Taproot was ready for deployment in October 2020, meaning all the technical details around its consensus rules had been implemented and had reached broad approval within the community, discussions on how to actually deploy it started to heat up. These discussions had been pretty low key up until that point.

Lots of proposals for activation mechanisms started floating around, and David Harding summarized them on the Bitcoin Wiki. In his article he explained some properties of BIP8, which at that time had some recent changes made in order to make it more flexible.

> *At the time this document is being written, BIP8 has been drafted based on lessons learned in 2017. One notable change following BIPs 9+148 is that forced activation is now based on block height rather than median time past; a second notable change is that forced activation is a boolean parameter chosen when a soft fork's activation parameters are set either for the initial deployment or updated in a later deployment.*
>
> *BIP8 without forced activation is very similar to BIP9 version bits with timeout and delay, with the only significant difference being BIP8's use of block heights compared to BIP9's use of median time past. This setting allows the attempt to fail (but it can be retried later).*
>
> *BIP8 with forced activation concludes with a mandatory signaling period where all blocks produced in compliance with its rules must signal readiness for the soft fork in a way that will trigger activation in an earlier deployment of the same soft fork with non-mandatory activation. In other words, if node version x is released without forced activation and, later, version y is released that successfully forces miners to begin signaling readiness within the same time period, both versions will begin enforcing the new consensus rules at the same time.*

This flexibility of the revised BIP8 proposal makes it possible to express some other ideas in terms of what they would look like using BIP8. This provides a common factor to use for categorizing many different proposals.

— David Harding – Taproot Activation Proposals on the Bitcoin Wiki (2020)

From this point forward the discussions became very heated, especially around whether `lockinontimeout` should be `true` (as in a user activated soft fork, referred to as "BIP8 with forced activation" by Harding) or `false` (as in a miner activated soft fork, referred to as "BIP8 without forced activation" by Harding).

Among the proposals listed, one of them was titled "Let's see what happens". For some reason, this proposal didn't get much traction until seven months later.

During those seven months, the discussion went on and it seemed like there was no way to reach broad consensus over which deployment mechanism to use. There were mainly two camps: one that preferred `lockinontimeout=true` (the UASF crowd) and the other one that preferred `lockinontimeout=false` (the "try and if it fails rethink" crowd). Since there was no overwhelming support for any of these options, the debate went in circles with seemingly no way forward. Some of these discussions were held on IRC, in a channel called ##taproot-activation, but on March 5th 2021, something changed:

```
06:42 < harding> roconnor: is somebody proposing BIP8(3m,
    ↪ false)?  I mentioned that the other day but I didn't
    ↪ see any responses.
 [...]
06:43 < willcl_ark_> Amusingly, I was just thinking to myself
    ↪  that, vs this, the SegWit activation was actually
```

```
      ↪ pretty straightforward: simply a LOT=false and if it
      ↪ fails a UASF.
06:43 < maybehuman> it's funny, "let's see what happens" (i.e
      ↪ . false, 3m) was a poular choice right at the beginning
      ↪  of this channel iirc
06:44 < roconnor> harding: I think I am.  I don't know how
      ↪ much that is worth.  Mostly I think it would be a
      ↪ widely acceptable configuration based on my
      ↪ understanding of everyone's concerns.
06:44 < willcl_ark_> maybehuman: becuase everybody actually
      ↪ wants this, even miners reckoned they could upgrade in
      ↪ about two weeks (or at least f2pool said that)
06:44 < roconnor> harding: BIP8(3m,false) with an extended
      ↪ lockin-period.
06:45 < harding> roconnor: oh, good.  It's been my favorite
      ↪ option since I first summarized the options on the wiki
      ↪  like seven months ago.
06:45 <@michaelfolkson> UASF wouldn't release (true,3m) but
      ↪ yeah Core could release (false, 3m)
06:45 < willcl_ark_> harding: It certainly seems like a good
      ↪ approach to me. _if_ that fails, then you can try an
      ↪ understand why, without wasting too much time
```

— *#taproot-activation IRC log*

The "let's see what happens" approach finally seemed to click in peoples' minds. This process would later be labeled as "Speedy Trial" due to its short signaling period. David Harding explains this idea to the broader community in an email to the Bitcoin-dev mailing list.

The earlier version of this proposal was documented over 200 days ago[3] and taproot's underlying code was merged into Bitcoin Core over 140 days ago.[4] If we had started Speedy Trial at the time taproot was merged (which is a bit unrealistic),

we would've either be less than two months away from having taproot or we would
have moved on to the next activation attempt over a month ago.

Instead, we've debated at length and don't appear to be any closer to what I
think is a widely acceptable solution than when the mailing list began discussing
post-segwit activation schemes over a year ago.[5] I think Speedy Trial is a way
to generate fast progress that will either end the debate (for now, if activation
is successful) or give us some actual data upon which to base future taproot
activation proposals.

— David Harding – on Bitcoin-dev mailing list

This deployment mechanism was refined over the course of two months
and then released in Bitcoin Core version 0.21.1. The miners quickly started
signaling for this upgrade moving the deployment state to LOCKED_IN, and
after a grace period the Taproot rules were activated mid-November 2021
in block 709632.

Future deployment mechanisms

Given the problems with the recent soft forks, Segwit and Taproot, it's not
clear how the next upgrade will be deployed. Speedy Trial was used to
deploy Taproot, but it was used to bridge the chasm between the UASF
and the MASF crowds, not because it has emerged as the best known
deployment mechanism.

Risks

During the activation of any fork, be it hard or soft, miner activated or user activated, there's the risk of a long-lasting chain split. A split that lingers for more than a few blocks can cause severe damage to the sentiment around Bitcoin as well as to its price. But above all, it would cause great confusion over what Bitcoin is. Is Bitcoin this chain or that chain?

The risk with a user activated soft fork is that the new rules get activated even if the majority of the hash power doesn't support them. This scenario would result in a long-lasting chain split, which would persist until the majority of the hash power adopts the new rules. It could be especially hard to incentivize miners to switch to the new chain if they had already mined blocks after the split on the old chain, because by switching branch they would be abandoning their own block rewards. However, it's worth mentioning a remarkable episode: in March 2013 a long-lasting split, explained in 2013-03-11 DB locks issue 0.7.2 - 0.8.0 (CVE-2013-3220), occurred due to an unintentional hard fork and, contrary to this incentive, two major mining pools made the decision to abandon their branch of the split in order to restore consensus.

On the other hand, the risk with a miner activated soft fork is a consequence of the fact that miners can engage in false signaling, which means that the actual share of the hash power that supports the change could be smaller than it looks. If the actual support doesn't comprise a majority of the hash power, we'd probably see a long-lasting chain split similar to the one described in the previous paragraph. This, or at least a similar issue, has happened in reality when BIP66 was deployed (see BIP66), but it got resolved within 6 blocks or so.

Costs of a split

Jimmy Song spoke about the costs associated with hard forks at Breaking Bitcoin in Paris, but much of what he said applies to a chain split due to a failed soft fork as well. He spoke about *negative externalities*, and defined them as the price someone else has to pay for your own actions.

> *The classic example of a negative externality is a factory. Maybe they are producing– maybe it's an oil refinery and they produce a good that is good for the economy but they also produce something that is a negative externality, like pollution. It's not just something that everyone has to pay for, to clean up, or suffer from. But it's also 2nd and 3rd order effects, like more traffic going towards the factory as a result of more workers that need to go there. You might also have- you might endanger some wildlife around there. It's not that everyone has to pay for the negative externalities, it might be specific people, like people who were previously using that road or animals that were near that factory, and they are also paying for the cost of that factory.*
>
> *— Jimmy Song – Socialized Costs Of Hard Forks at Breaking Bitcoin conference (2017)*

In the context of Bitcoin, he exemplifies negative externalities using Bitcoin Cash (bcash), which is a hard fork of Bitcoin created shortly prior to that conference in 2017. He categorizes the negative externalities of a hard fork into one-time costs and permanent costs.

Among the many examples of one-time costs, he mentions the ones incurred by exchanges.

> *So we have a bunch of exchanges and they had a lot of one-time costs that they had to pay. The first thing that happened is that deposits and withdrawals had to be halted for a day or two for these exchanges because they didn't know what*

would happen. Many of these exchanges had to dip into cold storage because their users were demanding bcash. It's part of their fidicuiary duty, they have to do that. You also have to audit the new software. This is something that we had to do at itbit. We want to spend bcash- how do we do it? We have to download electron cash? Does it have malware? We have to go and audit it. We had like 10 days to figure out if this was okay or not. And then you have to decide, are we going to just allow a one-time withdrawal, or are we going to list this new coin? For an exchange to lis ta new coin, it's not easy- there's all sorts of new procedures for cold storage, signing, deposits, withdrawals. Or you could just have this one-off event where you give them their bcash at some point and then you never think about it again. But that has its problems too. And finally, and whatever way you do it, withdrawals or listing– you are going to need new infrastructure to work with this token in some way, even if it's a one-time withdrawal. You need some way to give these tokens to your users. Again, short-notice. Right? No time to do this, has to be done quickly.

— Jimmy Song – Socialized Costs Of Hard Forks at Breaking Bitcoin conference (2017)

He also lists the one-time costs incurred by merchants, payment processors, wallets, miners, and users, as well as some of the permanent costs, for example privacy loss and a higher risk of reorgs.

Indeed, when a split happens and the chain with the most general rules becomes stronger than the chain with the stricter rules, a reorg will occur. This will have a severe impact on all transactions carried out in the wiped-out branch. For these reasons it's really important to try avoiding chain splits at all times.

Conclusion

Bitcoin grows and evolves with time. Different upgrade mechanisms have been used over the years and the learning curve is steep. More and more sophisticated and robust methods keep being invented, as we learn more about how the network reacts.

To keep Bitcoin in harmony, soft forks have proven to be the way forward, but the big question is still not fully answered: how do we safely deploy soft forks without causing discord?

6

ADVERSARIAL THINKING

This chapter addresses *adversarial thinking*, a mindset that focuses on what could go wrong and how adversaries might act. We start out by discussing Bitcoin's security assumptions and security model, after which we explain how ordinary users can improve their self-sovereignty and Bitcoin's full node decentralization by thinking adversarially. Then, we look into some actual threats to Bitcoin as well as into the adversary's mind. Lastly, we talk about the *axiom of resistance* which can help you understand why people are working on Bitcoin in the first place.

When discussing security within various systems, it's important to understand what the security assumptions are. A typical security assumption in Bitcoin is "the discrete logarithm problem is hard to solve", which, simply put, means it's practically impossible to find a private key that corresponds to a particular public key. Another pretty strong security assumption is that a majority of the network's hashpower is honest, meaning that they play by the rules. If these assumptions are proven wrong, then Bitcoin is in trouble.

In 2015 Andrew Poelstra gave a talk at the Scaling Bitcoin conference in Hong Kong, during which he analyzed Bitcoin's security assumptions. He starts by noticing that many systems disregard adversaries to some extent; for example, it's really hard to protect a building against all types of adversarial events. Instead, we generally accept the possibility that someone may burn the building down, and to some extent prevent this and other adversarial behaviors through law enforcement etc.

But online things are different:

> However, online we don't have this. We have pseudonymous and anonymous behavior, anyone can connect to everyone and hurt the system. If it's possible to adversarially hurt the system, then they will do it. We cannot assume they will be visible and that they will be caught.
>
> — Andrew Poelstra – Security Assumptions at Scaling Bitcoin Hong Kong (2015)

The consequence is that all known weaknesses in Bitcoin must somehow be taken care of, otherwise they will be exploited. After all, Bitcoin is the greatest honey pot in the world.

Poelstra goes on to mention how Bitcoin is a new kind of system; it's more nebulous than, for example, a signing protocol which has very clear-cut security assumptions.

On his personal blog, software engineer Jameson Lopp, dives into this:

> In reality, the bitcoin protocol was and is being built without a formally defined specification or security model. The best that we can do is to study the incentives

and behavior of actors within the system in order to better understand and attempt to describe it.

— *Jameson Lopp – Bitcoin's Security Model: A Deep Dive (2016)*

So, we have a system that seems to be working in practice, but that we can't formally prove to be secure. A proof is probably not possible due to the complexity of the system itself.

Not only for Bitcoin experts

The importance of adversarial thinking also extends to everyday Bitcoin users to some degree, not only to hardcore Bitcoin developers and experts. Ragnar Lifthasir mentions in a tweetstorm how simplistic narratives around Bitcoin - for example, "just HODL" - can be degrading to Bitcoin itself, and concludes by saying

> *To make Bitcoin and ourselves stronger we need to think like the software engineers who contribute to Bitcoin. They peer review, mercilessly seeking flaws. At their tech events they talk about every which way a proposal can fail. They think adversarially. They're conservative*
>
> — *Ragnar Lifthasir – Twitter (2020)*

He refers to these simplistic narratives as monomanias. Through this definition he's saying that by focusing on a single thing - for example, "just HODL"- you risk to overlook the arguably more important stuff, such as keeping your Bitcoin secure or doing your best to use Bitcoin in a trustless manner.

Threats

There are a lot of known weaknesses in Bitcoin, and many of them are actively being exploited. To get a glimpse of that, have a look at the Weaknesses page on Bitcoin wiki. There are mentioned a wide variety of problems, such as wallet theft and denial-of-service attacks.

> *If an attacker attempts to fill the network with clients that they control, you would then be very likely to connect only to attacker nodes. Although Bitcoin never uses a count of nodes for anything, completely isolating a node from the honest network can be helpful in the execution of other attacks.*
>
> — *Various authors – Bitcoin wiki*

This type of attack is called *Sybil attack*, and it occurs whenever a single entity controls multiple nodes in a network and uses them to appear as multiple entities.

As the quote also mentions, the Sybil attack is not effective on the Bitcoin network because there is no voting through nodes or other numerable entities, but rather through computing power (see Miner decentralization). Nonetheless, this flat structure leaves the system susceptible to other attacks. The Bitcoin wiki page also outlines other possible attacks, such as information hiding (often referred to as *eclipse attack*), and the way Bitcoin Core implements some heuristic countermeasures against such attacks.

The above are examples of real threats that need to be taken care of.

To better understand the adversary's mind, it might be helpful to get a glimpse into how they operate. A US government body named Office of Strategic Services, which operated during World War II and had among its

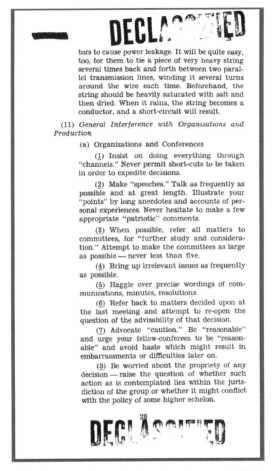

Figure 6.1: Excerpt from the Simple Sabotage Field Manual

purposes to conduct espionage, perform sabotage and spread propaganda, produced a manual for their personnel on how to properly sabotage the enemy. Its title was "Simple Sabotage Field Manual" and contained concrete tips on infiltrating the enemy to make their lives hard. The tips range from burning down warehouses to causing wear to drills in order to decrease the enemy's efficiency.

For example, there is a section about how an infiltrator can disrupt organizations. It's not hard to see how such tactics could be used to target the Bitcoin development process (see chapter Open Source), which is open for anyone to participate in. A dedicated attacker can keep stalling progress by endless concerns of irrelevant issues, haggle over precise wordings, and attempt to reiterate discussions that have already been comprehensively addressed. The attacker can also hire a troll army to multiply their own effectiveness; we can call this a social Sybil attack. Using a social Sybil attack, they can make it look like there's more resistance against a proposed change than there actually is.

This highlights how a determined state can and will do everything in its power to destroy the enemy, including breaking it down from the inside. Since Bitcoin is a form of money that competes with established fiat currencies, chances are that states will regard Bitcoin as an enemy.

Eric Voskuil writes on his Cryptoeconomics wiki page about what he calls the "axiom of resistance":

> *In other words there is an assumption that it is* possible *for a system to resist state control. This is not accepted as a fact but deemed to be a reasonable assumption, due to empirical study of behavior of similar systems, on which to base the system.*
>
> **One who does not accept the axiom of resistance is contemplating an entirely different system than Bitcoin.** *If one assumes it is* not possible *for a system to resist state controls, conclusions do not make sense in the context of Bitcoin - just as conclusions in spherical geometry contradict Euclidean. How can Bitcoin be permissionless or censorship-resistant without the axiom? The contradiction leads one to make obvious errors in an attempt to rationalize the conflict.*
>
> — *Eric Voskuil – Cryptoeconomics wiki (2017)*

What he's essentially saying is that only when one assumes it's possible to create a system that states can't control, is it meaningful to try.

This means that to work on Bitcoin you should accept the axiom of resistance, otherwise you'd better spend your time on other projects. Acknowledging that axiom helps you focusing your development efforts on the real problems at hand: coding around state-level adversaries. In other words, think adversarially.

Conclusion

A decentralized system can't have accountability outside the system itself, therefore Bitcoin must prevent malicious behavior more rigorously than traditional systems. Adversarial thinking is imperative in such a system.

To keep Bitcoin safe you need to know its enemies and their incentives. Most of the threats seem to boil down to nation states, who have enourmous economic power, through taxation and money printing. They probably won't give up their money printing privileges easily.

7

OPEN SOURCE

Bitcoin is built using open source software. In this chapter we analyze what this means, how maintenance of the software works, and how open source software in Bitcoin allows for permissionless development. We dip our toes into *selection cryptography*, which deals with the selection and use of libraries in cryptographic systems. The chapter includes a section about Bitcoin's review process, followed by another one on the ways Bitcoin developers get funded. The last section talks about how Bitcoin's open source culture can look really weird from the outside, and why this perceived weirdness is really a sign of good health.

Most Bitcoin softwares, and especially Bitcoin Core, is open source. This means that the source code of the software is made available to the general public for scrutiny, tinkering, modification, and redistribution. The definition of open source at https://opensource.org/osd includes, among others, the following important points:

Free Redistribution *The license shall not restrict any party from selling or giving away the software as a component of an aggregate software distribution containing programs from several different sources. The license shall not require a royalty or other fee for such sale.*

Source Code *The program must include source code, and must allow distribution in source code as well as compiled form. Where some form of a product is not distributed with source code, there must be a well-publicized means of obtaining the source code for no more than a reasonable reproduction cost, preferably downloading via the Internet without charge. The source code must be the preferred form in which a programmer would modify the program. Deliberately obfuscated source code is not allowed. Intermediate forms such as the output of a preprocessor or translator are not allowed.*

Derived Works *The license must allow modifications and derived works, and must allow them to be distributed under the same terms as the license of the original software.*

— The Open Source Definition – Open Source Initiative website

Bitcoin Core adheres to this definition by being distributed under the MIT License:

```
The MIT License (MIT)

Copyright (c) 2009-2022 The Bitcoin Core developers
Copyright (c) 2009-2022 Bitcoin Developers

Permission is hereby granted, free of charge, to any person obtaining a copy
of this software and associated documentation files (the "Software"), to deal
in the Software without restriction, including without limitation the rights
to use, copy, modify, merge, publish, distribute, sublicense, and/or sell
copies of the Software, and to permit persons to whom the Software is
furnished to do so, subject to the following conditions:

The above copyright notice and this permission notice shall be included in
all copies or substantial portions of the Software.
```

As noted in Don't trust, verify, it's important for users to be able to verify that the Bitcoin software they run "works as advertised". To do that, they must have unrestricted access to the source code of the software they wish to verify.

In the upcoming sections we dive into some other interesting aspects of open source software in Bitcoin.

Software maintenance

Bitcoin Core's source code is maintained in a Git repository hosted on GitHub. Anyone can clone that very repository without asking for any permission, and then inspect, build, or make changes to it locally. This means that there are many thousands of copies of the repository spread throughout the globe. These are all copies of the same repository, so what makes this specific GitHub Bitcoin Core repository so special? Technically it's not special at all, but socially it has become the focal point of Bitcoin development.

Bitcoin and security expert Jameson Lopp explains this very well in a blog post titled "Who Controls Bitcoin Core?":

> *Bitcoin Core is a focal point for development of the Bitcoin protocol rather than a point of command and control. If it ceased to exist for any reason, a new focal point would emerge—the technical communications platform upon which it's based (currently the GitHub repository) is a matter of convenience rather than one of definition / project integrity. In fact, we have already seen Bitcoin's focal point for development change platforms and even names!*
>
> *— Jameson Lopp – Who Controls Bitcoin Core? (2018)*

He goes on to explain how Bitcoin Core's software is maintained and secured against malicious code changes. The general takeaway from this full article is summarized at its very end:

No one controls Bitcoin.

No one controls the focal point for Bitcoin development.

— Jameson Lopp – Who Controls Bitcoin Core? (2018)

Bitcoin Core developer Eric Lombrozo talks further about the development process in his Medium post titled "The Bitcoin Core Merge Process".

Anyone can fork the code base repository and make arbitrary changes to their own repository. They can build a client from their own repository and run that instead if they want. They can also make binary builds for other people to run.

If someone wants to merge a change they've made in their own repository into Bitcoin Core, they can submit a pull request. Once submitted, anyone can review the changes and comment on them regardless of whether or not they have commit access to Bitcoin Core itself.

— Eric Lombrozo on Medium.com – The Bitcoin Core Merge Process (2017)

It should be noted that pull requests can take a very long time before being merged to the repository by maintainers, and that's usually due to a lack of review, see Review, which is often due to a lack of *reviewers*.

Lombrozo also talks about the process that surrounds consensus changes, but that's a bit beyond the scope of this chapter. See Upgrading for more information on how the Bitcoin protocol gets upgraded.

Permissionless development

We've established that anyone can write code for Bitcoin Core without asking for any permission, but not necessarily have it merged to the main Git repository. This affects any modification, from changing color schemes of the graphical user interface, to the way peer-to-peer messages are formatted, and even consensus rules, i.e. the set of rules that define a valid blockchain.

Probably equally important is that users are free to develop systems on top of Bitcoin, without asking for any permission. We've seen countless successful software projects that were built on top of Bitcoin, such as:

Lightning Network A payment network that allows for fast payment of very small amounts. It requires very few on-chain Bitcoin transactions. Various inter-operable implementations exist, such as Core Lightning, LND, Eclair, and Lightning Dev Kit.

CoinJoin Multiple parties collaborate to combine their payments into a single transaction to make address clustering (explained in Blockchain privacy) harder. Various implementations exist.

Sidechains This system can lock a coin on Bitcoin's blockchain in order to unlock it on some other blockchain. This allows for bitcoins to be moved to some other blockchain, namely a sidechain, so as to use the features available on that sidechain. Examples include Blockstream's Elements .

OpenTimestamps It allows you to timestamp a document on Bitcoin's blockchain in a private way. You can then use that timestamp to prove that a document must have existed prior to a certain time.

Without permissionless development, many of these projects would not have been possible. As stated in Neutrality, if developers had to ask for permission to build protocols on top of Bitcoin, only the protocols allowed by the central developer granting committee would be developed.

It is common for systems like the ones listed above to be themselves licensed as open source software, which in turn allows for people to contribute, re-use, or review their code without asking for any permission. Open source has become the gold standard of Bitcoin software licensing.

Pseudonymous development

Not having to ask for permission to develop Bitcoin software brings an interesting and important option to the table: you can write and publish code, in Bitcoin Core or any other open source project, without revealing your identity.

Many developers choose this option by operating under a pseudonym and trying to keep it detached from their true identity. The reasons for doing this can vary from developer to developer. One pseudonymous user is ZmnSCPxj. Among other projects, he contributes to Bitcoin Core and Core Lightning, one of several implementations of Lightning Network. He writes on his web page:

I am ZmnSCPxj, a randomly-generated Internet person. My pronouns are he/him/his.

I understand that humans instinctively desire to know my identity. However, I think my identity is largely immaterial, and prefer to be judged by my work.

If you are wondering whether to donate or not, and wondering what my cost of living or my income is, please understand that properly speaking, you should donate to me based on the utility you find my articles and my work on Bitcoin and the Lightning Network.

— ZmnSCPxj on his GitHub page

In his case, the reason for using a pseudonym is to be judged on his merits and not on who the person or persons behind the pseudonym is or are. Interestingly, he revealed in an article on CoinDesk that the pseudonym was created for a different reason.

My initial reason [for using a pseudonym] was simply that I was concerned [about] making a massive mistake; thus ZmnSCPxj was originally intended to be a disposable pseudonym that could be abandoned in such a case. However it seems to have garnered a mostly positive reputation, so I have retained it

— Many Bitcoin Developers Are Choosing to Use Pseudonyms – For Good Reason on CoinDesk (2021)

Using a pseudonym indeed allows you to speak more freely without putting your personal reputation at risk should you say something stupid or make some big mistake. As it turned out, his pseudonym got very reputable and in 2019 he even got a development grant, which is in itself a testament to Bitcoin's permissionless nature.

Arguably, the most well-known pseudonym in Bitcoin is Satoshi Nakamoto. It's unclear why he chose to be pseudonymous, but with hindsight it was probably a good decision for multiple reasons:

- As many people speculate that Nakamoto owns a lot of bitcoin, it's imperative for his financial and personal safety to keep his identity unknown.

- Since his identity is unknown, there is no possibility of prosecuting anyone, which gives various government authorities a hard time.

- There is no authoritative person to look up to, making Bitcoin more meritocratic and resilient against blackmailing.

Notice that these points don't just hold true for Satoshi Nakamoto, but for anyone working in Bitcoin or holding significant amounts of the currency, to varying degrees.

Selection cryptography

Open source developers often make use of open source libraries developed by other people. This is a natural and awesome part of any healthy ecosystem. But Bitcoin software deals with real money and, in light of this, developers need to be extra careful when choosing which third party libraries it should depend on.

In a philosophical talk about cryptography, Gregory Maxwell wants to redefine the term "cryptography" which he believes to be too narrow. He explains that fundamentally *information wants to be free*, and makes his definition of cryptography based on that:

> **Cryptography** *is the art and science we use to fight the fundamental nature of information, to bend it to our political and moral will, and to direct it to human ends against all chance and efforts to oppose it.*
>
> — *Gregory Maxwell – Bitcoin Selection Cryptography (2015)*

He then introduces the term *selection cryptography*, referred to as the art of selecting cryptographic tools, and explains why it is an important part of cryptography. It revolves around how to select cryptographic libraries, tools, and practices, or as he says "the cryptosystem of picking cryptosystems".

Using concrete examples, he shows how selection cryptography can easily go horribly wrong, and also proposes a list of questions you could ask yourself when practicing it. Below is a distilled version of that list:

1. Is the software intended for your purposes?

2. Are the cryptographic considerations being taken seriously?

3. The review process... is there one?

4. What is the experience of the authors?

5. Is the software documented?

6. Is the software portable?

7. Is the software tested?

8. Does the software adopt best practices?

While this is not the ultimate guide to success, it can be very helpful to go through these points when doing selection cryptography.

Due to the issues mentioned above by Maxwell, Bitcoin Core tries really hard to minimize its exposure to third party libraries. Of course, you can't eradicate all external dependencies, otherwise you'd have to write everything by yourself, from font rendering to implementation of system calls.

Review

This section is named "Review", rather than "Code review", because Bitcoin's security relies heavily on review at multiple levels, not just source code. Moreover, different ideas require review at different levels: a consensus rule change would require a deeper review at more levels compared to a color scheme change or a typo fix.

On its way to final adoption, an idea usually flows through several phases of discussion and review. Some of these phases are listed below:

1. An idea is posted on the Bitcoin-dev mailing list

2. The idea is formalized into a Bitcoin Improvement Proposal (BIP)

3. The BIP is implemented in a pull request (PR) to Bitcoin Core

4. Deployment mechanisms are discussed

5. Some competing deployment mechanisms are implemented in pull requests to Bitcoin Core

6. Pull requests are merged to the master branch

7. Users choose whether to use the software or not

At each of these phases people with different points of view and backgrounds review the available information, be it the source code, a BIP, or just a loosely described idea. The phases are usually not performed in any strict top-down manner, indeed multiple phases can happen simultaneously, and sometimes you go back and forth between them. Different people may also provide feedback during different phases.

One of the most prolific code reviewers on Bitcoin Core is Jon Atack. He wrote a blog post about how to review pull requests in Bitcoin Core. He emphasizes that a good code reviewer focuses on how to best add value.

> *As a newcomer, the goal is to try to add value, with friendliness and humility, while learning as much as possible.*
>
> *A good approach is to make it not about you, but rather "How can I best serve?"*
>
> — *Jon Atack – How to Review Pull Requests in Bitcoin Core (2020)*

He highlights the fact that review is a truly limiting factor in Bitcoin Core. Lots of good ideas get stuck in a limbo where no review occurs, pending. Notice that reviewing is not only beneficial to Bitcoin, but also a great way to learn about the software while providing value to it, at the same time. Atack's rule of thumb is to review 5-15 PRs before making any PR of your own. Again, your focus should be on how to best serve the community, not on how to get your own code merged. On top of this, he stresses the importance of doing review at the right level: is this the time for nits and typos, or does the developer need more of a conceptually-oriented review?

> *A useful first question when beginning a review can be, "What is most needed here at this time?" Answering this question requires experience and accumulated context, but it is a useful question in deciding how you can add the most value in the least time.*
>
> — *Jon Atack – How to Review Pull Requests in Bitcoin Core (2020)*

The second half of the post consists of some useful hands-on technical guidance on how to actually do the reviewing, and provides links to important documentation for further reading.

Bitcoin Core developer and code reviewer Gloria Zhao has written an article containing questions she usually asks herself during a review. She also states what she considers to be a good review.

> *I personally think a good review is one where I've asked myself a lot of pointed questions about the PR and been satisfied with the answers to them.*
> *...[snip]...*
> *Naturally, I start with conceptual questions, then approach-related questions, and then implementation questions. Generally, I personally think it's useless to leave C++ syntax-related comments on a draft PR, and would feel rude going back to "does this make sense" after the author has addressed 20+ of my code organization suggestions.*
>
> — *Gloria Zhao – Common PR Review Questions on GitHub (2022)*

Her idea that a good review should focus on what's most needed at a specific point in time aligns well with Jon Atack's advice. She proposes a list of questions that you may ask yourself at various levels of the review process, but stresses that this list is not in any way exhaustive nor a straight-out recipe. The list is illustrated with real-life examples from GitHub.

Funding

Lots of people work with Bitcoin open source development, either for Bitcoin Core or for other projects. Many do it in their spare time without getting any compensation, but some developers are also getting paid to do it.

Companies, individuals, and organizations who have an interest in Bitcoin's continued success can donate funds to developers, either directly or through organizations that in turn distribute the funds to individual developers. There are also a number of Bitcoin-focused companies that hire skilled developers to let them work full-time on Bitcoin.

Culture shock

People sometimes get the impression that there's a lot of infighting and endless heated debates among Bitcoin developers, and that they are incapable of making decisions.

For example, the Taproot deployment mechanism, described in Taproot upgrade - Speedy Trial, was discussed over a long period of time during which two "camps" formed. One wanted to "fail" the upgrade if miners hadn't overwhelmingly voted for the new rules after a certain moment, while the other wanted to enforce the rules after that moment no matter what. Michael Folkson summarizes the arguments from the two camps in an email to the Bitcoin-dev mailing list.

The debate went on seemingly forever, and it was really hard to see any consensus on this forming any time soon. This got people frustrated and as a result the heat intensified. Gregory Maxwell (as user nullc) worried on Reddit that the lengthy discussions would make the upgrade less safe.

> *At this juncture, additional waiting isn't adding more review and certainty. Instead, additional delay is sapping inertia and potentially increasing risk somewhat as people start forgetting details, delaying work on downstream usage (like wallet support), and not investing as much additional review effort as they would be investing if they felt confident about the activation timeframe.*
>
> *— Gregory Maxwell on Reddit – Is Taproot development moving too fast or too slow?*

Eventually, this dispute got resolved thanks to a new proposal by David Harding and Russel O'Connor called Speedy Trial, which entailed a comparatively shorter signaling period for miners to lock in activation of Taproot, or fail fast. If they activated it during that window of time, then Taproot would be deployed approximately 6 months later. This upgrade is covered in more detail in Upgrading.

Someone who's not used to Bitcoin's development process would probably think that these heated debates look awfully bad and even toxic. There are at least two factors that make them look bad, in some people's eyes:

- Compared to closed source companies, all debates happen in the open, unedited. A software company like Google would never let its employees debate proposed features in the open, indeed it would at most publish a statement about the company's stance on the subject. This makes companies look more harmonic compared to Bitcoin.

- Since Bitcoin is permissionless, anyone is allowed to voice their opinions. This is fundamentally different from a closed source company that has a handful of people with an opinion, usually like-minded people. The plethora of opinions expressed within Bitcoin is simply staggering compared to, for example, PayPal.

Most Bitcoin developers would argue that this openness brings about a good and healthy environment, and even that it is necessary for producing the best outcome.

As hinted in Threats, the second bullet above can be very beneficial but comes with a downside. An attacker could use stalling tactics, like the ones outlined in the Simple Sabotage Field Manual, to distort the decision making and development process.

Another thing worth mentioning is that, as noted in Selection cryptography, since Bitcoin is money and Bitcoin Core secures unfathomable amounts of money, security in this context is not taken lightly. This is why seasoned Bitcoin Core developers might appear very hard-headed, which attitude is usually warranted. Indeed, a feature with a weak rationale behind it is not going to be accepted. The same would happen if it broke the reproducible builds (described in Don't trust, verify), added new dependencies, or if the code didn't follow Bitcoin's best practices.

New (and old) developers can get frustrated by this. But, as is customary in open source software, you can always fork the repository, merge whatever you want to your own fork, and build and run your own binary.

Conclusion

Bitcoin Core and most other Bitcoin software is open source, which means that anyone is free to distribute, modify, and use the software as they please. The Bitcoin Core repository on GitHub is currently the focal point of Bitcoin development, but that status can change if people start to distrust its maintainers, or the website itself.

Open source allows for permissionless development in, and on top of Bitcoin. Whether you write code, review code or protocols; open source is what enables you to do it, pseudonomously or not.

The development process around Bitcoin is radically open, which can make Bitcoin look like a toxic and inefficient place, but that's what keeps Bitcoin resilient against malicious actors.

8

SCALING

In this chapter, we explore how Bitcoin does and does not scale. We start by looking at how people have reasoned about scaling in the past. Then, the bulk of this chapter explains various approaches to scaling Bitcoin, specifically vertical, horizontal, inward, and layered scaling. Each description is followed by considerations over whether the approach interferes with Bitcoin's value proposition.

In the Bitcoin space, different people ascribe different definitions to the word "scale". Some conceive it as the increase of the blockchain transaction capacity, others believe it equals to using the blockchain more efficiently, and others see it as the development of systems on top of Bitcoin.

In the context of Bitcoin, and for this book's purposes, we define scaling as *increasing Bitcoin's usage capacity without compromising its censorship resistance*. This definition encompasses several kinds of changes, for example:

- Making transaction inputs use fewer bytes

- Improving signature verification performance

- Making the peer-to-peer network use less bandwidth

- Transaction batching

- Layered architecture

We'll soon dive into different approaches to scaling, but let's start with a brief overview of Bitcoin's history within the context of scaling.

History

Scaling has been a focal point of discussion since the genesis of Bitcoin. The very first sentence of the very first email in response to Satoshi's announcement of the Bitcoin whitepaper on the Cryptography mailing list was indeed about scaling:

> Satoshi Nakamoto wrote:
> > I've been working on a new electronic cash system that's fully
> > peer-to-peer, with no trusted third party.
> >
> > The paper is available at:
> > http://www.bitcoin.org/bitcoin.pdf

We very, very much need such a system, but the way I understand your proposal, it does not seem to scale to the required size.

— James A. Donald and Satoshi Nakamoto – Cryptography mailing list (2008)

The conversation in itself might not be very interesting nor accurate, but it shows that scaling has been a concern from the very beginning.

Discussions over scaling reached their peak interest around 2015-2017, when there were many different ideas circulating about whether and how to increase the maximum block size limit. That was a rather uninteresting discussion about changing a parameter in the source code, a change that didn't fundamentally solve anything but pushed the problem of scaling further into the future, building technical debt.

In 2015, a conference called Scaling Bitcoin was held in Montreal, with a follow-up conference six months later in Hong Kong and thereafter in a number of other locations around the world. The focus was precisely on how to address scaling. Many Bitcoin developers and other enthusiasts gathered at these conferences to discuss various scaling issues and proposals. Most of these discussions didn't revolve around block size increases but on more long-term solutions.

After the Hong Kong conference in December 2015, Gregory Maxwell summarized his view on many of the issues that had been debated, starting off with some general scaling philosophy.

With the available technology, there are fundamental trade-offs between scale and decentralization. If the system is too costly people will be forced to trust third parties rather than independently enforcing the system's rules. If the Bitcoin blockchain's resource usage, relative to the available technology, is too great, Bitcoin loses its competitive advantages compared to legacy systems because

validation will be too costly (pricing out many users), forcing trust back into the system. If capacity is too low and our methods of transacting too inefficient, access to the chain for dispute resolution will be too costly, again pushing trust back into the system.

— *Gregory Maxwell – Capacity increases for the Bitcoin system (2015)*

He speaks about the trade-off between throughput and decentralization. If you allow for bigger blocks, you will push some people off the network because they won't have the resources to validate the blocks anymore. But on the other hand, if access to block space becomes more expensive, fewer people will be able to afford using it as a dispute resolution mechanism. In both cases, users are pushed towards trusted services.

He continues by summarizing the many approaches to scaling presented at the conference. Among them are more computationally efficient signature verifications, *segregated witness* including a block size limit change, a more space-efficient block propagation mechanism, and building protocols on top of Bitcoin in layers. Many of these approaches have since been implemented.

Scaling approaches

As hinted above, scaling Bitcoin doesn't necessarily have to be about increasing the block size limit or other limits. We now go through some general approaches to scaling, some of which don't suffer from the throughput-decentralization trade-off mentioned in the previous section.

Vertical scaling

Vertical scaling is the process of increasing the computing resources of the machines processing data. In the context of Bitcoin, these latter would be the full nodes, namely the machines that validate the blockchain on behalf of their users.

The most commonly discussed technique for vertical scaling in Bitcoin is the increase in the block size limit. This would require some full nodes to upgrade their hardware to keep up with the increasing computational demands. The downside is that it happens at the cost of centralization, as was discussed in the previous section and more in depth in Full node decentralization.

Besides the negative effects on full node decentralization, vertical scaling might also negatively impact Bitcoin's mining decentralization (explained in Miner decentralization) and security in less obvious ways. Let's have a look at how miners "should" operate. Say a miner mines a block at height 7 and publishes that block on the Bitcoin network. It will take some time for this block to reach broad acceptance, which is mainly due to two factors:

- Transfer of the block between peers takes time due to bandwidth limitations.

- Validation of the block takes time.

While block 7 is being propagated through the network, many miners are still mining on top of block 6 because they haven't received and validated block 7 yet. During this time, if any of these miners finds a new block at height 7, there will be two competing blocks at that height. There can only be one block at height 7 (or any other height), which means one of the two candidates must become stale.

In short, stale blocks happen because it takes time for each block to propagate, and the longer propagation takes, the higher the probability of stale blocks.

Suppose that the block size limit is lifted and that the average block size increases substantially. Blocks would then propagate slower across the network due to bandwidth limitations and verification time. An increase in propagation time will also increase the chances of stale blocks.

Miners don't like to have their blocks staled because they'll lose their block reward, so they will do whatever they can to avoid this scenario. The measures they can take include:

- Postponing the validation of an incoming block, also known as *validationless mining*, further discussed in Splits due to validationless mining. Miners can just check the block header's proof-of-work and mine on top of it, while in the meantime they download the full block and validate it.

- Connecting to a mining pool with greater bandwidth and connectivity.

Validationless mining further undermines full node decentralization, as the miner resorts to trusting incoming blocks, at least temporarily. It also hurts security to some degree because a portion of the network's computing power is potentially building on an invalid blockchain, instead of building on the strongest and valid chain.

The second bullet point has a negative effect on miner decentralization, see Miner decentralization, because usually the pools with the best network connectivity and bandwidth are also the largest, causing miners to gravitate towards a few big pools.

Horizontal scaling

Horizontal scaling refers to techniques that divide the workload across multiple machines. While this is a prevalent scaling approach among popular websites and databases, it's not easily done in Bitcoin.

Many people refer to this Bitcoin scaling approach as *sharding*. Basically, it consists in letting each full node verify just a portion of the blockchain. Peter Todd has put a lot of thought into the concept of sharding. He wrote a blog post explaining sharding in general terms, and also presenting his own idea called *treechains*. The article is a difficult read, but Todd makes some points that are quite digestible.

> *In sharded systems the "full node defense" doesn't work, at least directly. The whole point is that not everyone has all the data, so you have to decide what happens when it's not available.*
>
> — *Peter Todd – Why Scaling Bitcoin With Sharding Is Very Hard (2015)*

Then he presents various ideas on how to tackle sharding, or horizontal scaling. Towards the end of the post he concludes:

> *There's a big problem though: holy !@#$ is the above complex compared to Bitcoin! Even the "kiddy" version of sharding - my linearization scheme rather than zk-SNARKS - is probably one or two orders of magnitude more complex than using the Bitcoin protocol is right now, yet right now a huge % of the companies in this space seem to have thrown their hands up and used centralized API providers instead.*

Actually implementing the above and getting it into the hands of end-users won't be easy.

On the other hand, decentralization isn't cheap: using PayPal is one or two orders of magnitude simpler than the Bitcoin protocol.

— Peter Todd – Why Scaling Bitcoin With Sharding Is Very Hard (2015)

The conclusion he makes is that sharding *might* be technically possible, but it would come at the cost of tremendous complexity. Given that many users already find Bitcoin too complex and prefer to use centralized services instead, it's going to be hard to convince them to use something even more complex.

Inward scaling

While horizontal and vertical scaling have historically worked out well in centralized systems like databases and web servers, they don't seem to be suitable for a decentralized network like Bitcoin due to their centralizing effects.

An approach that gets far too little appreciation is what we can call *inward scaling,* which translates into "do more with less". It refers to the ongoing work constantly done by many developers to optimize the algorithms already in place, so that we can do more within the existing limits of the system.

The improvements that have been achieved through inward scaling are impressive, to say the least. To give you a general idea of the improvements over the years, Jameson Lopp has run benchmark tests on blockchain synchronization, comparing many different versions of Bitcoin Core going back to version 0.8.

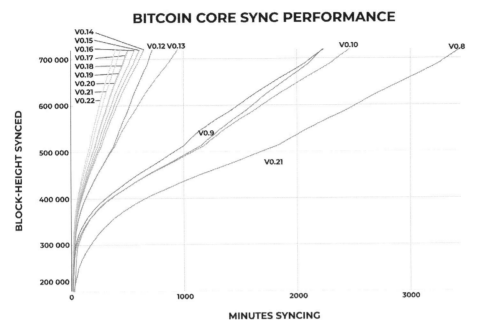

Figure 8.1: Initial block download performance of various versions of Bitcoin Core. On the Y-axis is the block height synced and on the X-axis is the time it took to sync to that height.

The different lines represent different versions of Bitcoin Core. The left-most line is the latest, i.e. version 0.22, which was released in September 2021 and took 396 minutes to fully sync. The rightmost one is version 0.8 from November 2013, which took 3452 minutes. All of this - roughly 10x - improvement is due to inward scaling.

The improvements could be categorized as either saving space (RAM, disk, bandwidth, etc.) or saving computational power. Both categories contribute to the improvements in the diagram above.

A good example of computational improvement can be found in the libsecp256k1 library, which, among other things, implements the cryptographic primitives needed to make and verify digital signatures.

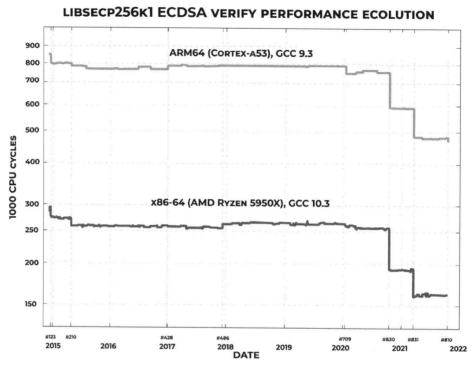

Figure 8.2: Performance of signature verification over time, with significant pull requests marked on the timeline.

Pieter Wuille is one of the contributors to this library, and he wrote a Twitter thread showcasing the performance improvements achieved through various pull requests.

The graph shows the trend for two different 64-bit CPU types, namely ARM and x86. The difference in performance is due to the more specialized instructions available on x86 compared to the ARM architecture, which has fewer and more generic instructions. However, the general trend is the same for both architectures. Note that the Y-axis is logarithmic, which makes the improvements look less impressive than they actually are.

Input	Native Segwit	Taproot (P2TR)		
		key path	script path	
Single-sig	68.5 vB P2WPKH	57.5 vB	--	--
2-of-3	104.5 vB P2WSH		82.75 vB MuSig leaf	107.5 vB 2-of-2 leaf

Output	Native Segwit	Taproot (P2TR)
Single-sig	31 B P2WPKH	43 B
2-of-3	43 B P2WSH	

created by @murchandamus

Figure 8.3: Space savings for different spending types, Taproot and legacy versions.

There are also several good examples of space-saving improvements that contributed to performance enhancement. In a Medium blog post about Taproot's contribution to saving space, user Murch compares how much block space a 2-of-3 threshold signature would require, using Taproot in various ways as well as not using it at all.

A 2-of-3 multisig using native Segwit would require a total of 104.5+43 vB = 147.5 vB, whereas the most space-conservative use of Taproot would require only 57.5+43 vB = 100.5 vB in the standard use case. At worst and in rare cases, like when a standard signer is not available for some reason, Taproot would use 107.5+43 vB = 150.5 vB. You don't have to understand all the details, but this should give you an idea of how developers think about saving space - every little byte counts.

Apart from inward scaling in Bitcoin software, there are some ways in which users can contribute to inward scaling, too. They can make their transactions more intelligently to save on transaction fees while simultaneously decreasing their footprints on full node requirements. Two commonly used techniques toward such goal are called transaction batching and output consolidation.

The idea with transaction batching is to combine multiple payments into one single transaction, instead of making one transaction per payment. This can save you a lot of fees, and at the same time reduce the block space load.

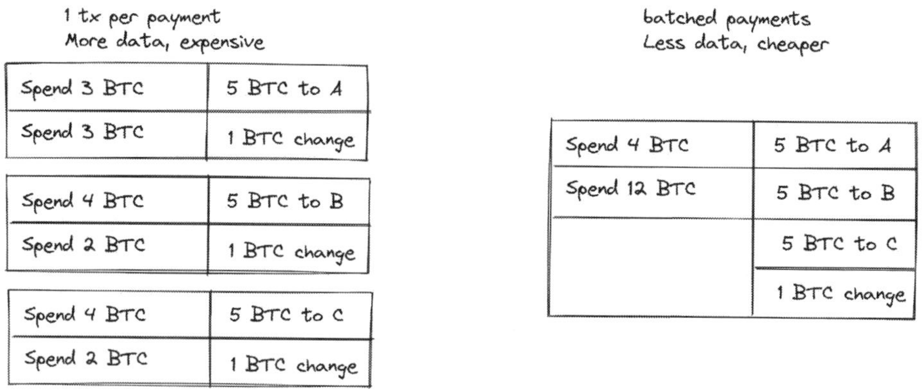

Figure 8.4: Transaction batching combines multiple payments into a single transaction to save on fees.

Output consolidation refers to taking advantage of periods of low demand for block space to combine multiple outputs into a single output. This can reduce your fee cost later, when you'll need to make a payment while the demand for block space is high (See Figure 8.5).

It may not be obvious how output consolidation contributes to inward scaling. After all, the total amount of blockchain data is even slightly increased with this method. Nonetheless, the UTXO set, i.e. the database that keeps track of who owns which coins, shrinks because you spend more

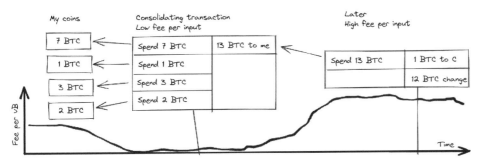

Figure 8.5: Output consolidation. Melt your coins into one big coin when fees are low to save fees later.

UTXOs than you create. This alleviates the burden for full nodes to maintain their UTXO sets.

Unfortunately, however, these two techniques of *UTXO management* could be bad for your own or your payees' privacy. In the batching case, each payee will know that all the batched outputs are from you to other payees (except possibly the change). In the UTXO consolidation case, you will reveal that the outputs you consolidate belong to the same wallet. So you may have to make a trade-off between cost efficiency and privacy.

Layered scaling

The most impactful approach to scaling is probably layering. The general idea behind layering is that a protocol can settle payments between users without adding transactions to the blockchain. This was already discussed briefly in Trustlessness and Privacy measures.

A layered protocol begins with two or more people agreeing on a start transaction that's put on the blockchain, as illustrated in Figure 8.6.

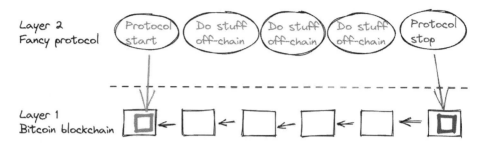

Figure 8.6: A typical layer 2 protocol on top of Bitcoin, layer 1.

How this start transaction is created varies between protocols, but a common theme is that the participants create an unsigned start transaction and a number of pre-signed punishment transactions, that spend the output of the start transaction in various ways. Subsequently, the start transaction is fully signed and published to the blockchain, and the punishment transactions can be fully signed and published to punish a misbehaving party. This incentivizes the participants to keep their promises so that the protocol can work in a trustless way.

Once the start transaction is on the blockchain, the protocol can do what it's supposed to do. For instance, it could do super fast payments between participants, implement some privacy-enhancing techniques, or do more advanced scripting that would not be supported by the Bitcoin blockchain.

We won't detail how specific protocols work, but as you can see in Figure 8.6, the blockchain is rarely used during the protocol's life cycle. All the juicy action happens *off-chain*. We've seen how this can be a win for privacy if done right, but it can also be an advantage for scalability.

In a Reddit post titled "A trip to the moon requires a rocket with multiple stages or otherwise the rocket equation will eat your lunch... packing everyone in clown-car style into a trebuchet and hoping for success is right

out.", Gregory Maxwell explains why layering is our best shot at getting
Bitcoin to scale by orders of magnitudes.

He starts by emphasizing the fallacy in viewing Visa or Mastercard as
Bitcoin's main competitors and highlighting how increasing the maximum
block size is a bad approach to meet said competition. Then he talks about
how to make some real difference by using layers.

> *So-- Does that mean that Bitcoin can't be a big winner as a payments technology?
> No. But to reach the kind of capacity required to serve the payments needs of the
> world we must work more intelligently.*
>
> *From its very beginning Bitcoin was design to incorporate layers in secure ways
> through its smart contracting capability (What, do you think that was just put
> there so people could wax-philosophic about meaningless "DAOs"?). In effect we
> will use the Bitcoin system as a highly accessible and perfectly trustworthy robotic
> judge and conduct most of our business outside of the court room-- but transact in
> such a way that if something goes wrong we have all the evidence and established
> agreements so we can be confident that the robotic court will make it right. (Geek
> sidebar: If this seems impossible, go read this old post on transaction cut-through)*
>
> *This is possible precisely because of the core properties of Bitcoin. A censorable or
> reversible base system is not very suitable to build powerful upper layer transaction
> processing on top of... and if the underlying asset isn't sound, there is little point
> in transacting with it at all.*
>
> *— Gregory Maxwell – r/Bitcoin on Reddit (2016)*

The analogy with the judge is quite illustrative of how layering works: this
judge must be incorruptible and never change her mind, otherwise the
layers above Bitcoin's base layer will not work reliably.

He continues by making a point about centralized services. There's usually no problem with trusting a central server with trivial amounts of Bitcoin to get things done: that's also layered scaling.

Many years have passed since Maxwell wrote the piece above, and his words still stand correct. The success of the Lightning Network proves that layering is indeed a way forward to increase the utility of Bitcoin.

Conclusion

We've discussed various ways through which one might want to scale Bitcoin, increase Bitcoin's usage capacity. Scaling has been a concern in Bitcoin since its very early days.

We know today that Bitcoin doesn't scale well vertically ("buy bigger hardware") or horizontally ("verify only parts of the data"), but rather inward ("do more with less") and in layers ("build protocols on top of Bitcoin").

9

WHEN SHIT HITS THE FAN

Bitcoin is built by people. People write the software, and people then run this software. When a security vulnerability or a severe bug is discovered - is there really a distinction between the two? - it's always discovered by people, flesh and blood. This chapter contemplates what people do, should, and shouldn't do when shit hits the fan. The first section explains the term *responsible disclosure*, which refers to how someone who discovers a vulnerability can act responsibly to help minimize the damage from it. The rest of the chapter takes you on a tour through some of the most severe vulnerabilities discovered over the years, and how they were handled by developers, miners, and users. Things were not as rigorous in Bitcoin's early childhood as they are today.

Responsible disclosure

Imagine you discover a bug in Bitcoin Core, a bug that allows anyone to remotely shut down a Bitcoin Core node by using some specially crafted network messages. Imagine also you are not malicious and would like this issue to remain unexploited. What do you do? If you remain silent about it, someone else will probably discover the issue, and you can't be sure that person won't be malicious.

When a security issue is discovered, the person discovering it should employ *responsible disclosure* which is a term often used among Bitcoin developers. The term is explained on Wikipedia:

> *Developers of hardware and software often require time and resources to repair their mistakes. Often, it is ethical hackers who find these vulnerabilities.[1] Hackers and computer security scientists have the opinion that it is their social responsibility to make the public aware of vulnerabilities. Hiding problems could cause a feeling of false security. To avoid this, the involved parties coordinate and negotiate a reasonable period of time for repairing the vulnerability. Depending on the potential impact of the vulnerability, the expected time needed for an emergency fix or workaround to be developed and applied and other factors, this period may vary between a few days and several months.*
>
> *— Wikipedia – Responsible disclosure article*

This means that if you find a security issue, you should report this to the team responsible for the system. But what does this mean in the context of Bitcoin? As noted in Software maintenance, no one controls Bitcoin, but there's currently a focal point for Bitcoin development, namely the Bitcoin Core Github repository. The maintainers of said repository are responsible for the code in it, but they're not responsible for the system as a whole - no one is. Nevertheless, the general best practice is to send an email to security@bitcoincore.org.

In an email thread titled "Responsible disclosure of bugs" from 2017, Anthony Towns tried to summarize what he perceived to be the current best practices.   He had collected inputs from several sources and different people to inform his view on the subject.

- *Vulnerabilities should be reported via security at bitcoincore.org [0]*

- *A critical issue (that can be exploited immediately or is already being exploited causing large harm) will be dealt with by:*

  - *a released patch ASAP*

  - *wide notification of the need to upgrade (or to disable affected systems)*

  - *minimal disclosure of the actual problem, to delay attacks [1] [2]*

- *A non-critical vulnerability (because it is difficult or expensive to exploit) will be dealt with by:*

  - *patch and review undertaken in the ordinary flow of development*

  - *backport of a fix or workaround from master to the current released version [2]*

- *Devs will attempt to ensure that publication of the fix does not reveal the nature of the vulnerability by providing the proposed fix to experienced devs who have not been informed of the vulnerability, telling them that it fixes a vulnerability, and asking them to identify the vulnerability. [2]*

- *Devs may recommend other bitcoin implementations adopt vulnerability fixes prior to the fix being released and widely deployed, if they can do so without revealing the vulnerability; eg, if the fix has significant performance benefits that would justify its inclusion. [3]*

- *Prior to a vulnerability becoming public, devs will generally recommend to friendly altcoin devs that they should catch up with fixes. But this is only after the fixes are widely deployed in the bitcoin network. [4]*

- *Devs will generally not notify altcoin developers who have behaved in a hostile manner (eg, using vulnerabilities to attack others, or who violate embargoes). [5]*

- *Bitcoin devs won't disclose vulnerability details until >80% of bitcoin nodes have deployed the fixes. Vulnerability discovers are encouraged and requested to follow the same policy. [1] [6]*

— Anthony Towns in thread "'Responsible disclosure of bugs'" – Bitcoin-dev email list (2017)

This list displays how careful one must be when publishing patches for Bitcoin, since the patch itself might give away the vulnerability. The fourth bullet is particularly interesting as it explains how to test whether a patch has been disguised well enough. Indeed, if a few really experienced developers can't spot the vulnerability even knowing that the patch fixes one, it will probably be really hard for others to discover it.

The thread that led to this email was discussing whether, when, and how to disclose vulnerabilities to altcoins and other implementations of Bitcoin. There is no clear answer here. "Helping the good guys" seems like the sensible thing to do, but who decides who they are and where does one draw the line? Bryan Bishop argued that helping altcoins and even scamcoins defend themselves against security exploits was a moral duty.

> *It's not enough to defend bitcoin and its users from active threats, there is a more general responsibility to defend all kinds of users and different software from many kinds of threats in whatever forms, even if folks are using stupid and insecure software that you personally don't maintain or contribute to or advocate for. Handling knowledge of a vulnerability is a delicate matter and you might be receiving knowledge with more serious direct or indirect impact than originally described.*
>
> *— Bryan Bishop in thread "'Responsible disclosure of bugs'" – Bitcoin-dev email list (2017)*

Also leading up to Town's email above was a post by Gregory Maxwell, in which he argued that security vulnerabilities could be more severe than they appear.

> *I've multiple time seen a hard to exploit issue turn out to be trivial when you find the right trick, or a minor dos issue turn our to far more serious.*
>
> *Simple performance bugs, expertly deployed, can potentially be used to carve up the network--- miner A and exchange B go in one partition, everyone else in another.. and doublespend.*
>
> *And so on. So while I absolutely do agree that different things should and can be handled differently, it is not always so clear cut. It's prudent to treat things as more severe than you know them to be.*
>
> — *Gregory Maxwell in thread "'Responsible disclosure of bugs'" – Bitcoin-dev email list (2017)*

So, even if a vulnerability seems hard to exploit, it might be best to assume that it's easily exploitable and you just haven't figured out how yet.

He also mentions how "it's somewhat incorrect to call this thread anything about disclosure, this thread is not about disclosure. Disclosure is when you tell the vendor. This thread is about publication and that has very different implications. Publication is when you're sure you've told the prospective attackers". This last observation concerning the distinction between disclosure and publication is an important one. The easy part is responsible disclosure; the hard part is sensible publishing.

Traumatic childhood

Bitcoin started out as a one-man (at least that's what its creator's pseudonym suggests) project, and bitcoin had initially little to no value. As such, vulnerabilities and bug fixes were not as rigorously handled as they are today.

The Bitcoin wiki has a list of common vulnerabilities and exposures (CVEs) that Bitcoin has gone through. This section constitutes a little exposé of some of the security issues and incidents from the early years of Bitcoin. We won't cover them all, but we selected a few that we find especially interesting.

2010-07-28: Spend anyone's coins (CVE-2010-5141)

On July 28, 2010, a pseudonymous person by the name ArtForz discovered a bug in version 0.3.4 that would let anyone take coins from anyone else. ArtForz *responsibly* reported this to Satoshi Nakamoto and to another Bitcoin developer named Gavin Andresen.

The problem was that the script operator `OP_RETURN` would simply exit the program execution, so if the scriptPubKey was `<pubkey> OP_CHECKSIG` and scriptSig was `OP_1 OP_RETURN`, the part of the program in the script-PubKey would never execute. The only thing that would happen would be for 1 to be put on the stack and then `OP_RETURN` would cause the program to exit. Any non-zero value on top of the stack after the program has executed means that the spending condition is fulfilled. Since the top stack element 1 is non-zero, the spending would be OK.

This was the code for handling of OP_RETURN:

```
case OP_RETURN:
{
    pc = pend;
}
break;
```

The effect of `pc = pend;` was for the rest of the program to get skipped, meaning that any locking script in scriptPubKey would be ignored. The fix consisted in changing the meaning of OP_RETURN so that it immediately failed, instead.

```
case OP_RETURN:
{
    return false;
}
break;
```

Satoshi made this change locally and built an executable binary with version 0.3.5 from it. Then he posted on Bitcointalk forum "*** ALERT *** Upgrade to 0.3.5 ASAP", urging users to install this binary version of his, without presenting the source code for it.

> *Please upgrade to 0.3.5 ASAP! We fixed an implementation bug where it was possible that bogus transactions could be accepted. Do not accept Bitcoin transactions as payment until you upgrade to version 0.3.5!*
>
> *— Satoshi Nakamoto – Bitcointalk forum (2010)*

The original message was later edited and is no longer available in its full form. The above snippet is from a quoting answer. Some users tried Satoshi's binary, but ran into issues with it. Shortly after, Satoshi wrote:

Haven't had time to update the SVN yet. Wait for 0.3.6, I'm building it now. You can shut down your node in the meantime.

— Satoshi Nakamoto – Bitcointalk forum (2010)

And 35 minutes later, he wrote

SVN is updated with version 0.3.6.

Uploading Windows build of 0.3.6 to Sourceforge now, then will rebuild linux.

— Satoshi Nakamoto – Bitcointalk forum (2010)

At this point he also seemed to have updated the original post to mention 0.3.6 instead of 0.3.5:

Please upgrade to 0.3.6 ASAP! We fixed an implementation bug where it was possible that bogus transactions could be displayed as accepted. Do not accept Bitcoin transactions as payment until you upgrade to version 0.3.6!

If you can't upgrade to 0.3.6 right away, it's best to shut down your Bitcoin node until you do.

Also in 0.3.6, faster hashing:

- midstate cache optimisation thanks to tcatm

- Crypto++ ASM SHA-256 thanks to BlackEye

Total generating speedup 2.4x faster.

Download:

http://sourceforge.net/projects/bitcoin/files/Bitcoin/bitcoin-0.3.6/

Windows and Linux users: if you got 0.3.5 you still need to upgrade to 0.3.6.

— Satoshi Nakamoto – Bitcointalk forum (2010)

Note the difference in the characterization of the problem from the first message: "could be displayed as accepted" vs "could be accepted". Maybe Satoshi downplayed the severity of the bug in his communication so as not to draw too much attention to the actual issue. Anyhow, people upgraded to 0.3.6 and it worked as expected. This particular issue was resolved, amazingly, with no bitcoin losses.

Satoshi's message also described some performance optimization for mining. It's unclear why that was included in a critical security fix, it's possible that the purpose was to obfuscate the real issue. However, it seems more likely that he just released whatever was on the head of the development branch of the Subversion repository, with the security fix added to it.

At that time, there weren't nearly as many users as there are today, and bitcoin's value was close to zero. If this bug response was played out today, it would be considered a complete shit-show for multiple reasons:

- Satoshi made a binary-only release of 0.3.5 containing the fix. No patch or code was provided, maybe as a measure to obfuscate the issue.

- 0.3.5 didn't even work.

- The fix in 0.3.6 was actually a hard fork, as explained in Historic upgrades.

Another debatable thing is whether it's good or bad that users were asked to shut down their nodes. This wouldn't be doable today, but at that time lots of users were actively following the forums for updates and were usually on top of things. Given that it was possible to do this, it might have been a sensible thing to do.

2010-08-15 Combined output overflow (CVE-2010-5139)

In mid-August 2010, Bitcointalk forum user jgarzik, a.k.a. Jeff Garzik, discovered that a certain transaction at block height 74638 had two outputs of unusually high value:

The "value out" in this block #74638 is quite strange:

```
. . .
    "out" : [
        {
            "value" : 92233720368.54277039,
            "scriptPubKey" : "OP_DUP OP_HASH160 0
                ↪ xB7A73EB128D7EA3D388DB12418302A1CBAD5E890
                ↪ OP_EQUALVERIFY OP_CHECKSIG"
        },
        {
            "value" : 92233720368.54277039,
            "scriptPubKey" : "OP_DUP OP_HASH160 0
                ↪ x151275508C66F89DEC2C5F43B6F9CBE0B5C4722C
                ↪ OP_EQUALVERIFY OP_CHECKSIG"
        }
    ]
. . .
```

92233720368.54277039 BTC? Is that UINT64_MAX, I wonder?

— *Jeff Garzik – Bitcointalk forum (2010)*

Presumably, there was a bug causing two int64 (not uint64, as Garzik supposed) outputs' sum to overflow to a negative value -0.00997538 BTC. Whatever the sum of the inputs, the "sum" of the outputs would be smaller, making this transaction OK according to the code at the time.

In this case, the bug had been disclosed and published through an actual exploit. An unfortunate outcome of this was that about 2x92 billion bitcoin had been created, which severely diluted the money supply of around 3.7 million coins that existed at that time.

In a related thread, Satoshi posted that he'd appreciate it if people stopped mining (or *generating*, as they called it back then).

> *It would help if people stop generating. We will probably need to re-do a branch around the current one, and the less you generate the faster that will be.*
>
> *A first patch will be in SVN rev 132. It's not uploaded yet. I'm pushing some other misc changes out of the way first, then I'll upload the patch for this.*
>
> — *Satoshi Nakamoto – Bitcointalk forum (2010)*

His plan was to make a soft fork to make transactions like the one discussed here invalid, thus invalidating the blocks (especially block 74638) that contained such transactions. Less than an hour later, he committed a patch in revision 132 of the Subversion repository and posted to the forum describing what he thought users should do:

> *Patch is uploaded to SVN rev 132!*
>
> *For now, recommended steps:*
>
> *1) Shut down.*
>
> *2) Download knightmb's blk files. (replace your blk0001.dat and blkindex.dat files)*
>
> *3) Upgrade.*
>
> *4) It should start out with less than 74000 blocks. Let it redownload the rest.*
>
> *If you don't want to use knightmb's files, you could just delete your blk*.dat files, but it's going to be a lot of load on the network if everyone is downloading the whole block index at once.*
>
> *I'll build releases shortly.*

He wanted people to download block data from a specific user, namely knightmb, who had published his blockchain as it appeared on his disk, the files blkXXXX.dat and blkindex.dat. The reason for downloading the blockchain data this way, as opposed to synchronizing from scratch, was to reduce network bandwidth bottlenecks.

There was a big caveat with this: the data users would download from knightmb weren't verified by the Bitcoin software at startup. The blkindex.dat file contained the UTXO set, and the software would accept any data therein as if it had already verified it. knightmb could have manipulated the data to give himself or anyone else some bitcoins.

Again, people seemed to go along with this, and the reversal of the invalid block and its successors was successful. Miners started working on a new successor to block 74637 and, according to the block's timestamp, a successor appeared at 23:53 UTC, about 6 hours after the issue was discovered. At 08:10 the following day, on August 16, around block 74689, the new chain had overtaken the old chain, therefore all non-upgraded nodes reorged to follow the new chain. This is the deepest reorg - 52 blocks - in Bitcoin's history.

Compared to the OP_RETURN issue, this issue was handled in a somewhat cleaner way:

- No binary-only patch release

- The released software worked as intended

- No hard fork

Users were asked to stop mining during this issue as well. We can discuss whether this is a good idea or not, but imagine you're a miner and you're convinced that any blocks on top of the bad block will eventually get wiped out in a deep reorg: why would you waste resources on mining doomed blocks?

You might also think that it's a bit fishy to do as suggested by Nakamoto and download the blockchain, including the UTXO set, from a random dude's hard drive. If so, you're right: that is fishy. But, given the circumstances, this emergency response was a sensible one.

There's an important difference between this case and the previous OP_RETURN case: this issue was exploited in the wild, and thus a fix could be made more straightforward. In the case of OP_RETURN, they had to obfuscate the fix and make public statements that didn't directly reveal what the issue was.

2013-03-11 DB locks issue 0.7.2 - 0.8.0 (CVE-2013-3220)

A very interesting an educationally valuable issue surfaced in March 2013. It appeared that the blockchain had split (although the word "fork" is used in the quote below) after block 225429. The details of this incident were reported in BIP50. The summary says:

> *A block that had a larger number of total transaction inputs than previously seen was mined and broadcasted. Bitcoin 0.8 nodes were able to handle this, but some pre-0.8 Bitcoin nodes rejected it, causing an unexpected fork of the blockchain. The pre-0.8-incompatible chain (from here on, the 0.8 chain) at that point had around 60% of the mining hash power ensuring the split did not automatically resolve*

(as would have occurred if the pre-0.8 chain outpaced the 0.8 chain in total work, forcing 0.8 nodes to reorganise to the pre-0.8 chain).

In order to restore a canonical chain as soon as possible, BTCGuild and Slush downgraded their Bitcoin 0.8 nodes to 0.7 so their pools would also reject the larger block. This placed majority hashpower on the chain without the larger block, thus eventually causing the 0.8 nodes to reorganise to the pre-0.8 chain.

— *Various Bitcoin Core developers – BIP50 (2013)*

The quick action that the mining pools BTCGuild and Slush took was imperative in this emergency. They were able to tip the majority of the hash power over to the pre-0.8 branch of the split, and thus help restore consensus. This gave developers the time to figure out a sustainable fix.

What's also very interesting in this issue is that version 0.7.2 was incompatible with itself, as was the case with prior versions too. This is explained in the Root cause section of BIP50:

With the insufficiently high BDB lock configuration, it implicitly had become a network consensus rule determining block validity (albeit an inconsistent and unsafe rule, since the lock usage could vary from node to node).

— *Various Bitcoin Core developers – BIP50 (2013)*

In short, the issue is that the number of database locks the Bitcoin Core software needs to verify a block is not deterministic. One node might need X locks while another node might need X+1 locks. The nodes also have a limit on how many locks Bitcoin can take. If the number of locks needed exceeds the limit, the block will be considered invalid. So if X+1 exceeds the limit but not X, then the two nodes will split the blockchain and disagree on which branch is valid.

The solution chosen, apart from the immediate actions taken by the two pools to restore consensus, was to

- limit the blocks in terms of both size and locks needed on version 0.8.1

- patch old versions (0.7.2 and some older ones) with the same new rules, and increase the global lock limit.

Except for the increased global lock limit in the second bullet, these rules were implemented temporarily for a pre-determined amount of time. The plan was to remove these limits once most nodes had upgraded.

This soft fork dramatically reduced the risk of consensus failure, and a few months later, on May 15, the temporary rules were deactivated in concert across the network. Note that this deactivation was in effect a hard fork, but it was not contentious. Furthermore, it was released along with the preceding soft fork, so people running the soft-forked software were well aware that a hard fork would follow it. Therefore, the vast majority of nodes remained in consensus when the hard fork got activated. Unfortunately, though, a few nodes that didn't upgrade were lost in the process.

One might wonder if this would be doable today. The mining landscape is more complex today, and, depending on the hash power on each side of the split, it might be hard to roll out a patch such as the one in BIP50 quickly enough. It'd probably be hard to convince miners on the "wrong" branch to let go of their block rewards.

BIP66

BIP66 is interesting because it highlights the importance of

- good selection cryptography

- responsible disclosure

- deployment without revealing the vulnerability

- mining on top of verified blocks

BIP66 was a proposal to tighten up the rules for signature encodings in Bitcoin Script. The motivation was to be able to parse signatures with software or libraries other than OpenSSL and even recent versions of OpenSSL. OpenSSL is a library for general purpose cryptography that Bitcoin Core used at that time.

The BIP activated on July 4, 2015. However, while the above is true, BIP66 also fixes a much more severe issue not mentioned in the BIP.

The vulnerability

The full disclosure of this issue was published on July 28 2015 by Pieter Wuille in an email to the Bitcoin-dev mailing list:

> Hello all,
>
> I'd like to disclose a vulnerability I discovered in September 2014, which became unexploitable when BIP66's 95% threshold was reached earlier this month.
> ## Short description:
> A specially-crafted transaction could have forked the blockchain between nodes:

- *using OpenSSL on a 32-bit systems and on 64-bit Windows systems*

- *using OpenSSL on non-Windows 64-bit systems (Linux, OSX, ...)*

- *using some non-OpenSSL codebases for parsing signatures*

— *Pieter Wuille on Bitcoin-dev mailing list – Disclosure: consensus bug indirectly solved by BIP66 (2015)*

The email further lays out the details about how the issue got discovered and more exactly what caused it. At the end, he submits a timeline of the events, and we will replay some of the most important ones here. Some of them have, as illustrated by Figure 9.1, already been described.

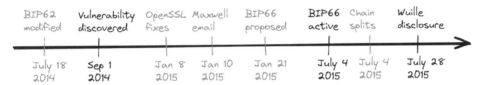

Figure 9.1: Timeline of events surrounding BIP66. Items in black have been explained above.

Before discovery

Without anyone knowing about the issue, it could have been resolved by the now widthdrawn BIP62, which was a proposal to reduce the possibilities of transaction malleability. Among the proposed changes in BIP62 were tightening of the consensus rules for the encoding of signatures, or "strict DER encoding". Pieter Wuille proposed some tweaks to the BIP in July 2014, that would have solved the issue:

- *2014-Jul-18: In order to make Bitcoin's signature encoding rules not depend on OpenSSL's specific parser, I modified the BIP62 proposal to have its strict*

DER signatures requirement also apply to version 1 transactions. No non-DER signatures were being mined into blocks anymore at the time, so this was assumed to not have any impact. See https://github.com/bitcoin/bips/ pull/90 and http://lists.linuxfoundation.org/pipermail/bitcoin-dev/2014-July/ 006299.html. Unknown at the time, but if deployed this would have solved the vulnerability.

— Pieter Wuille on Bitcoin-dev mailing list – Disclosure: consensus bug indirectly solved by BIP66 (2015)

Due to the breadth of this BIP, which covered substantially more than just "strict DER encoding", it was constantly changing and never got near deployment. The BIP was later withdrawn because Segregated Witness, BIP141, solved transaction malleability in a different and more complete way.

After discovery

OpenSSL released new versions of their software with patches that, if used in Bitcoin since the beginning, would have solved the issue. However, using any new version of OpenSSL only in a new release of Bitcoin Core would make matters worse. Gregory Maxwell explains this in another email thread in January 2015:

While for most applications it is generally acceptable to eagerly reject some signatures, Bitcoin is a consensus system where all participants must generally agree on the exact validity or invalidity of the input data. In a sense, consistency is more important than "correctness".

...

The patches above, however, only fix one symptom of the general problem: relying on software not designed or distributed for consensus use (in particular OpenSSL) for consensus-normative behavior. Therefore, as an incremental improvement, I propose a targeted soft-fork to enforce strict DER compliance soon, utilizing a subset of BIP62.

— Gregory Maxwell on OpenSSL upgrade – Bitcoin-dev mailing list

He points out that using code that's not intended for use in consensus systems poses serious risks, and proposes that Bitcoin implements strict DER encoding. This is a very clear example of the importance of good selection cryptography, a term we discussed in Selection cryptography.

These events might give you the impression that Gregory Maxwell knew about the vulnerability Pieter Wuille later published, but wanted to help sneak in a fix disguised as a precaution measure, without drawing too much attention to the actual problem. It might be so, but it's purely speculation.

Then, as proposed by Maxwell, BIP66 was created as a subset of BIP62 that specified only strict DER encoding. This BIP was apparently broadly accepted and deployed in July, albeit two blockchain splits ironically occurred due to *validationless mining*. These splits are discussed in the next section.

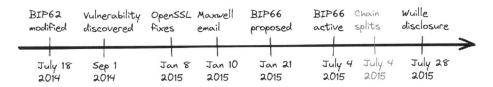

A key takeaway from this is that BIPs should be more or less *atomic*, meaning that they should be complete enough to provide something useful or solve a specific problem, but small enough to allow for broad support among users. The more stuff you put into a BIP, the smaller the chance of acceptance.

Splits due to validationless mining

Unfortunately, the story of BIP66 didn't end there. When BIP66 was activated, it turned out quite messy because some miners didn't verify the blocks they were trying to extend. This is called validationless mining, or SPV-mining (as in Simplified Payment Verification). An alert message was sent out to Bitcoin nodes with a link to a web page describing the issue.

> *Early morning on 4 July 2015, the 950/1000 (95%) threshold was reached. Shortly thereafter, a small miner (part of the non-upgraded 5%) mined an invalid block– as was an expected occurrence. Unfortunately, it turned out that roughly half the network hash rate was mining without fully validating blocks (called SPV mining), and built new blocks on top of that invalid block.*
>
> — Bitcoin Core developers – Alert information on bitcoin.org (2015)

The alert page instructed people to wait for 30 additional confirmations than they normally would in case they were using older versions of Bitcoin Core.

The split mentioned above occurred on 2015-07-04 at 02:10 UTC after block height 363730. This issue got resolved at 03:50 the same day, after 6 invalid blocks had been mined. Unfortunately, the same issue happened again the next day, i.e. on 2015-07-05 at 21:50, but this time the invalid branch only lasted 3 blocks.

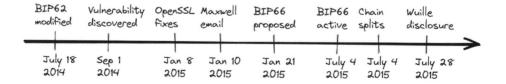

The events that led up to BIP66, its deployment, and the aftermath are a very good case study for how careful Bitcoin developers have to be. A few key takeaways from BIP66:

- The balance between openness and not publishing a vulnerability is a delicate one.

- Deploying fixes for non-published vulnerabilities is a tricky game to play.

- Retaining consensus is hard.

- Software not intended for consensus systems are generally risky.

- BIPs should be somewhat atomic.

Conclusion

Bitcoin has bugs. People discovering bugs are encouraged to disclose them responsibly to Bitcoin developers, so they can fix the bug without revealing it publicly. Ideally, the bug fix can be disguised as a performace improvement, or some other smoke screen.

We've looked at some of the more severe issues that's surfaced through the years, and how they were handled. Some were discovered publicly through exploits while other were responsibly disclosed and could be fixed before malicious actors had a chance to exploit them.

DISCUSSION QUESTIONS

These discussion questions are not just a recap of the content in "Bitcoin development philosophy", they are meant to encourage you to research further so make sure to go out and explore.

Decentralization

- Decentralization is hard. Why do we go through all of this hassle to make it work? Could we opt for a hybrid approach, where some parts are centralized and others aren't?

- Does decentralization introduce the double spending problem, or does the double spending problem require decentralization? How did Satoshi solve the double spending problem?

- In which aspects is Bitcoin still most prone to censorship, and why is censorship such a bad thing? Are there any arguments in favor of censorship?

- It is stated that Bitcoin is permissionless. Are there any other payment methods you could consider permissionless?

Trustlessness

- Trustlessness is often a spectrum, not binary. Which aspects of Bitcoin are rather trustless, and which typically involve a higher level of trust? Can they be mitigated?

- You want to run a full node to be able to fully validate all transactions. You download Bitcoin Core from https://bitcoin.org/en/download. Where did you place trust, and where are you fully trustless?

- Can you build a trustless system on top of a trusted system?

Privacy

- What are some important benefits a user gains when he maintains good privacy when interacting with Bitcoin? What are some altruistic benefits for the network?

- How does reusing addresses affect your privacy?

- Bitcoin uses a UTXO model, whereas some alternative cryptocurrencies use an account model. What are the implications of this choice on privacy?

Finite supply

- What is the relation between Bitcoin's finite supply and its coin issuance through the coinbase transaction? What is the relation between coin issuance and security budget, and how are they at odds?

- What parameters could Satoshi have tweaked to change Bitcoin's supply cap? What would change if he had decided to cap the supply to 1 million? What about 1 trillion?

- Why are some people advocating for an increase in Bitcoin supply? Do you think this will happen?

Upgrading

- What is Speedy Trial and why was it necessary to activate Taproot?

- Why do we need such a high percentage of miners to upgrade in a softfork? Why is the threshold not just 51%?

Adversarial thinking

- What is a sybil attack, and what makes a decentralized network so prone to it?

- Why is it important that all players in the Bitcoin network - and not just developers - think adversarially?

Open source

- Only a handful of maintainers have the necessary GitHub permissions to merge code into into the Bitcoin Core repository. Isn't that at odds with a permissionless network?

- Is the open source development process prone to a sybil attack? If so, how would you counter that?

- What are the benefits and downsides of relying on third party open source libraries, and what is the approach taken with Bitcoin Core?

- In which ways do we need review beyond just code review? How to determine how much review is enough?

- How do we ensure there will always be sufficient people with expertise working on Bitcoin? What happens when there aren't, and how do we asses their integrity and intentions?

Scaling

- It is argued that sharding offers scaling benefits at the cost of complexity. Why should we or should we not adopt technological improvements because they are difficult to understand, even if they appear technologically sound?

- What are some examples of inward scaling methods introduced in Bitcoin?

- Why is vertical scaling much more difficult in a decentralized system? What about horizontal scaling?

- We don't seem to be anywhere near having consensus on how we could onboard the entire world onto Bitcoin. Shouldn't Satoshi have at least thought of a path of getting there, before mining the first block in 2009?

- How would you classify (vertical, horizontal, inward, or not a scaling technique) each of the following: sharding, blocksize increase, SegWit, SPV nodes, centralized exchanges, Lightning Network, block interval decrease, Taproot, sidechains

About the Book

Bitcoin Development Philosophy is a comprehensive guide aimed at developers who have a foundational understanding of Bitcoin concepts and processes such as Proof-of-Work, block building, and the transaction life cycle. This book delves into the intricacies of Bitcoin's design trade-offs and philosophy, offering insights and context that help developers absorb over a decade of development lessons and debates.

The book is organized into several chapters, each focusing on pivotal topics within Bitcoin, such as decentralization, trustlessness, privacy, finite supply, and scaling, among others. Every chapter is enriched with links and QR codes leading to recommended articles or videos, written by seasoned Bitcoin developers. It not only provides practical insights but also encourages independent exploration and critical thinking about contradictory ideas prevalent in the Bitcoin community.

About the Authors

Kalle Rosenbaum, the main author, is a seasoned software developer with extensive experience in Bitcoin-related development since 2015. He is the author of Grokking Bitcoin and has been a pivotal figure in educating developers about Bitcoin.

Linnéa Rosenbaum, the co-author, holds a Ph.D. in Electronic Systems and has a rich background in firmware and software development. She is the Swedish translator of The Little Bitcoin Book and co-translator of The Bitcoin Standard, contributing significantly to the dissemination of knowledge about Bitcoin in Sweden. Their combined expertise and passion for Bitcoin have been instrumental in creating a guide that is insightful, comprehensive, and enlightening.

SOURCES

A complete overview of all the sources in this book can be accessed via https://bitcoindevphilosophy.com/sources/sources.html.

Made in the USA
Columbia, SC
21 September 2024